THE DVD BOOK OF
MANCHESTER
CITY

Written by David Clayton

THE DVD BOOK OF
MANCHESTER CITY

This edition first published in the UK in 2007
By Green Umbrella Publishing

© Green Umbrella Publishing 2007

www.greenumbrella.co.uk

Publishers Jules Gammond, Vanessa Gardner

Printed and bound in China

ISBN 13 978-1-905828-68-5

Contents

Academy

IN 1998, THE BLUES LAUNCHED the Manchester City Academy, based close to the club's former Maine Road stadium at Platt Lane. A more professional set-up with strict criteria set by various official organisations, the main focus was to coach as many young hopefuls through to the first team as possible. In 2007, Daniel Sturridge became the 21st graduate from the Academy to play first-team football – an incredible achievement by Academy director Jim Cassell and his coaches. Five of the youngsters have gone on to win full caps for their country, too, with Shaun Wright-Phillips – the first player to go from the Academy into the senior side – Micah Richards and Joey Barton all playing for England, and Stephen Ireland and Stephen Elliot (now at Sunderland) playing for Ireland. The full list of graduates who've played for the first team at City is: Joey Barton, Lee Croft, Jon D'Laryea, Terry Dunfield, Stephen Elliott, Dickson Etuhu, Willo Flood, Stephen Ireland, Tyrone Mears, Michael Johnson, Stephen Jordan, Chris Killen, Leon Mike, Ishmael Miller, Nedum Onuoha, Micah Richards, Chris Shuker, Danny Sturridge, Glenn Whelan, Bradley Wright-Phillips, Shaun Wright-Phillips.

Allison

BRASH, LOUD-MOUTHED, ARRO-gant but brilliant. Malcolm Allison was a one of a kind football coach who, it is widely acknowledged, was many years ahead of his field. Innovative and tactically brilliant, Allison was the perfect foil for the more steadying, fatherly figure of manager Joe Mercer. In July 1965, Mercer approached upcoming Plymouth Argyle boss Allison and offered him the position of head coach at Maine Road. With a desire to work at a higher level, he accepted and so began one of the most successful manage-ment teams English football has ever seen. Though the pair were like chalk and cheese, together they were a dream team, steering the Blues to the Second Division Champions in their first season and within two years, City were crowned First Division Champions for only the second time in the club's history.

Allison was often in trouble with the authorities for his touch-line outbursts and was banned time and time again by the FA – if Big Mal had some-thing to say, he said it and to hell with the consequences.

Coveted by a host of other top clubs – Leeds and Juventus among their number – he felt he

FAR LEFT Joey Barton, 2007

MIDDLE Bradley Wright-Phillips during the FA Cup fourth round match between Manchester City and Wigan Athletic, 2006

LEFT Malcolm Allison holds the Football League Cup in the air, 1970

BELOW Malcolm
Allison emerges into
the stadium, 1973

needed to be his own man and in 1972 was given the chance to prove himself by City. Just nine months later, the flamboyant champagne-drinking, cigar-smoking manager had left for Crystal Palace, believing he could no longer motivate the City players. In fact, his managing skills could never match his ability on the training ground and in July 1979 he returned for a second spell at the club, but it proved nothing short of disastrous and he was sacked in October 1980. He once said: 'I used to shout that I was the greatest coach in the world.' Few, especially the players and fans who were around in the late 1960s, would disagree.

Anglo-Italian Cup

INITIATED IN 1969 AS A CONTEST for English and Italian league teams, the primary objective was to reward Swindon Town, who were the English League Cup winners in 1969. However, as a Third Division club they were not allowed to enter the Fairs' Cup (Later UEFA Cup). Not a trophy fondly remembered by City fans, the Blues played in this odd competition on only one occasion in September 1970. The criteria for the competition was the English winners of the League Cup meeting the winners of the Italian Cup over a two-legged basis, but the fate of the tournament looked bleak from the word go. City played Bologna away in the first leg, losing 1-0 in front of a 28,000 crowd. The return leg at Maine Road ended in a 2-2 draw with City's goals scored by George Heslop and Francis Lee in front of a respectable 25,843 fans. Bologna took the glory and that was the sum total of the Blues' involvement. Travel costs, poor crowds and disciplinary problems eventually saw the demise of the competition, but it did make a brief reappearance in the 1990s, only to encounter the same difficulties as before.

ABOVE The team that won the League Cup and the European Cup Winners' Cup, 1970

RIGHT One of the groundstaff watches a training session, 1951

Ardwick FC

WHEN THE SKIPPER OF GORTON Football Club discovered an ideal patch of ground for his team to make their home on, the club upped sticks and moved the short distance to Ardwick. With a new home and new neighbourhood, it was agreed that it made sense to change the name from Gorton FC to Ardwick FC and a new club was formed. Under manager Lawrence Furniss, the profile of the team began to rise and

Ardwick twice won the Manchester Cup, beating Newton Heath 1-0 in 1891, who were later to become cross-town rivals Manchester United. However, beset by financial problems, in 1893-94 the club was forced into bankruptcy and in 1894 the phoenix that arose from the ashes of Ardwick FC was Manchester City Football Club, thanks in no small way to secretary Joshua Parlby. City would at least continue to play in Ardwick at their dilapidated Hyde Road ground, until 1923 when the club relocated to Maine Road.

Attendances

THE 1934 FA CUP TIE BETWEEN Manchester City and Stoke City still holds the record for the biggest crowd in a competitive English match outside games played at Wembley Stadium. Some 84,569 people crammed into Maine Road that day to see Eric Brook's solitary goal send City through to the next round. A decade earlier, 76,166 fans packed Maine Road to watch City draw 0-0 with Cardiff City. As late as 1956, two crowds of 76,129 and 70,640 watched the Blues take on Everton and Liverpool respectively in the FA Cup. City would win the trophy that season having no doubt been buoyed by the tremendous support they had been

receiving. The Blues' record League crowd was set on February 23, 1935 when 79,491 fans watched City and Arsenal slug out a 1-1 draw.

The lowest crowd on record is 3,000 in 1924 when Nottingham Forest were the visitors and they took full advantage of the sparse surrounds by beating City 3-1. A poor City side attracted just 8,015 people in January, 1964 for a Second Division clash with Swindon Town, the post-war record low.

ABOVE Manchester City fans serenade their team with a chorus of Blue Moon

LEFT Part of the crowd of supporters at a match between Clapton Orient and Manchester City, 1926

Ballet on Ice

ON DECEMBER 9 1967, MOST OF Britain awoke to find a blanket of snow and many football fans correctly assumed their team's game would be called off. City were due to take on Tottenham at Maine Road and having built up a head of steam in the league in recent weeks, the Blues were desperate for the match to go ahead and fortunately, the referee passed the pitch fit to play.

City boss Joe Mercer decided to let his players warm up an hour before kick-off to acclimatise to the slippery conditions and it proved to be one of his many managerial masterstrokes. Realising the snow was beginning to freeze over, skipper Tony Book suggested his teammates unscrew their studs to expose a small screw – just enough to grip the treacherous conditions with.

The Blues came out and played with sure-footed grace that had Spurs on the

rack virtually from the word go, but still fell behind to an early Jimmy Greaves strike. As the snow began to fall again, City stormed back in almost blizzard-like conditions to score goals through Colin Bell, Mike Summerbee, Tony Coleman and Neil Young. After the match, legendary Everton striker, Dixie Dean, watching from the stands, described the Blues as one of the best sides he had ever seen and the press were so taken by City's performance that it became known as the Ballet on Ice.

Bananas

THERE HAVE BEEN many occasions when City have driven their supporters bananas so it was perhaps apt that an inflatable form of the tropical fruit should become the supporters' unofficial mascot during a period when football desperately needed some good press.

Following tragedies at Heysel Stadium in Belgium and the Bradford City fire, football's image had never been bleaker, so when one man, City fan Frank Newton, borrowed an inflatable banana from a friend and took it to a match, he couldn't have imagined the positive effect it would have over the next couple of years.

The craze at Maine Road caught on quickly and soon there were dozens of bananas around the ground on match days, and it wasn't long before other City fans started bringing their own take on the blow-up craze.

Match days during the 1988-89 season were colourful affairs, especially on the Kippax terrace and the Blues' faithful were rightly praised by the media for bringing some much-needed humour back to a bit of a dull period for the club and football in general. Play fights ensued between an inflated Frankenstein and a green Dinosaur and often the inflatables proved more entertaining than the football on offer. There were even rumours Fyffe's were considering a shirt sponsorship deal!

The craze caught on around the country and supporters at other clubs had their own varied themes, one of the best being Stoke City and their legions of Pink Panthers, Grimsby Town and their 'Harry the Haddocks' and Norwich City with their yellow canaries. Bananas can still be seen at City home and away games even today, almost 20 years on.

LEFT Manchester City v Tottenham Hotspur, 1967

Barnes

LONG BEFORE CRISTIANO RONALDO was even a twinkle in his father's eye, Manchester City had a sleight-of-foot winger who could tie a defender in

knots with the drop of a shoulder or a clever dummy. His name was Peter Barnes and the blond haired teenager burst onto the scene in the mid-Seventies and became a household name by scoring City's first goal in the 1976 League Cup final against Newcastle.

Barnes came from great stock and his father, Ken, was a legend at Maine Road in the 1950s and was famously dubbed 'the best uncapped wing-half in England'. Barnes senior later became City's chief scout but on this occasion, he had to look no further than his own back garden to find an outstanding talent in waiting.

One of the best out-and-out wingers to ever play for Manchester City, he terrorized defences for three seasons and was one of the originators of the step-over dummy. Influenced by the likes of Mike Summerbee and Rodney Marsh, whom he had watched from the terraces as a boy, Barnes had an ability to cross the ball from seemingly impossible angles and won 14 England caps during his time with City, before rashly being sold by Malcolm Allison in 1979. He returned for a largely forgettable second spell in 1987.

Bell

UNDOUBTEDLY THE MOST POP-
ular player ever to wear the shirt of
Manchester City, when Blues' fans talk
about 'The King', they are referring to
only one man – Colin Bell. With his
limitless energy, skill and all-round
ability, he was the beating heart of the
most successful City team of all time.
He was, quite simply, probably the most
complete player the club has ever had
and a tremendous natural athlete. Bell
was signed by Joe Mercer from Bury in
March 1966 after the club finally
managed to raise the necessary £45,000
transfer fee. They faced stiff competition from Sunderland and it took
Malcolm Allison's vocal assassination of
the youngster to put off the hordes of
other scouts watching from the Gigg
Lane stands. As England's most
respected coach reeled off one made-up
deficiency about Bell after another, it
must have cast doubts in lesser mortals'
minds and the player completed his
move to Maine Road, making the
No 8 shirt his own from 1966 to
mid-November 1975.

Nicknamed 'Nijinsky', after another

famous thoroughbred of the era, a race-
horse, Bell went on to win 48 caps for
England – a record for a City player –
and also scored a memorable goal
against World Champions Brazil in Rio.
Along with Mike Summerbee and
Francis Lee, he completed what became
known as The Holy Trinity and the trio
drove the Blues to success after success.

RIGHT Bell, about to
win one of his 48
England caps, 1974

the edge of the box. Bell stated that he had been in three minds as to whether he was going to cut inside, shoot from a distance or go around Buchan. He chose the latter and would regret it for the rest of his life. With severe damage to his knee ligaments, Bell somehow battled back to play a handful of games for the Blues and after his testimonial in December 1978 – a Manchester v Merseyside match – he was forced to retire in August 1979. Just how many more trophies City might have won with a fit Bell in the team is

Bell was in his prime when he suffered a serious knee injury during a Manchester derby, when United's Martin Buchan scythed him down on debatable, but they almost certainly would have added a league title to the cabinet in 1977. A Maine Road legend in every sense of the word.

Benarbia

OCCASIONALLY, A CLUB AND A player come together and the end result is a magical concoction that despite being relatively short, stays in the memory for many years after.

Algerian International Ali Benarbia's brief time at Manchester City is one such example. Twice voted French Player of the Year, Benarbia was out of contract with French side Paris St Germain and travelled to England for a trial with Sunderland. The skilful midfielder felt poorly treated on Weirside, and left the club intending to return to Paris, stopping off to see a friend at City's Carrington training ground on his way back. Manager Kevin Keegan was well aware of Benarbia's exciting talent after he had twice scored against Keegan's Newcastle while at Monaco and he chatted with the player over lunch, offering him a trial in the process. It took Keegan about five minutes to offer Benarbia a deal and the player was more than happy to accept. Blessed with almost telepathic vision, Benarbia became an instant crowd favourite and as a free transfer, he represented a fantastic piece of business by Keegan. He was the creative genius behind the Blues' memorable 2001/02 campaign in which City scored 124 goals. Ali was unanimously voted Player of the Year by the City fans after a string of incredible performances in midfield but at 33, he was at the wrong end of his career. He stayed another year before moving to Qatar side Al-Rayyan in 2003, leaving many happy memories behind.

LEFT Ali Benarbia in action during a match between Leeds United and Manchester City, 2002

Bond

RIGHT (L–R)
Manchester City
manager John Bond
and chairman Peter
Swailes enjoying each
other's company in the
directors' box

JOHN BOND ARRIVED AT MAINE Road in October 1980 to pick up the pieces of Malcolm Allison's whirlwind second stay as City boss. Having achieved success at Bournemouth and Norwich City, the flamboyant but highly regarded Bond left the tranquil surrounds of Carrow Road for the crisis-torn Blues. Within weeks, Bond had transformed a doomed side into a team worthy of a top three place.

Few managers have had such an instant effect on a side and after watching his troops from the stand lose 1-0 to Birmingham, a result that left City bottom with no wins in 12, he inspired the players to produce a stirring 3-1 win over Spurs just four days later and the juggernaut was off and running. Only a linesman's flag denied City a place in the League Cup final that season and only a coat of paint saved Tottenham Hotspur in the first FA Cup final as Bond's City became the nations' premier cup team. Signings such as Gerry Gow, Bobby McDonald and Tommy Hutchison combined to play the best football of their careers and inspire the rest of the side to greater heights, and the side that had looked liked relegation bankers ended in twelfth spot.

The following campaign saw the arrival of Trevor Francis for £1.2 million and caused great excitement among supporters. The Blues went into the New Year at the top of the table, with many believing the seemingly impossible quest for the league title might just happen. It didn't, and a dramatic slump in form would eventually see City finish tenth. Bond lasted just over five months of the 1982-83 season with his magic aura fading by the week and he resigned after a 4-0 FA Cup fourth-round defeat at Brighton and Hove Albion and four months later the Blues were relegated.

Book

FEW MEN HAVE SERVED MAN-chester City with greater distinction than Tony Book, first as captain of the greatest City team of all time, then as manager from 1974 to 1979. 'Skip' joined City from Plymouth Argyle in 1966 for £17,000. Malcolm Allison, who had managed Book at both Bath and Plymouth, persuaded Joe Mercer that, despite Book being 30 years old, he was one of the finest defenders in the country. All this from a player who had just two years earlier been playing for non-league Bath and bricklaying part-time.

Book was made captain and was soon lifting the league championship, League Cup and FA Cup as well as being voted City's first ever Player of the Year in 1967. One of the quickest defenders around, George Best is quoted as listing Book as his most difficult opponent and he was also voted joint Footballer of the Year in 1969 as his fellow professionals acknowledged his tremendous achieve-ments over the past season or so.

Malcolm Allison said Book was one of the best defenders he'd ever seen and few who saw him play would disagree with that view. Tony captained City to another trophy in 1970, the European Cup Winners' Cup and he officially retired in 1974 in order to become assistant to Ron Saunders. He became manager not long after, taking City to League Cup glory at Wembley in 1976 and within a point of the First Division title in 1976-77, before being replaced, ironically, by Malcolm Allison in 1979. He later became part of the backroom staff at Maine Road for several more years. As a captain and as a manager, Book gave the Blues tremendous serv-ice, which stretched over an incredible 30 years.

RIGHT Tony Book (left) and goalkeeper Joe Corrigan walk out onto the pitch before their game against Ipswich Town, 1970

Busby

IT WAS AT MANCHESTER CITY, NOT
Manchester United, that the great Sir
Matt Busby first made his name in
England. The young Lanarkshire-born
Scot was all set to relocate to America
with his widowed mother until City
boss Peter Hodge persuaded him to stay
and sign for the Blues in 1928, changing
his life forever. Originally an inside-
forward, City adapted Busby into a
classy half-back and in 1933 he went on
to win his one and only Scotland cap.
He helped City win the FA Cup in 1934,
having been a Wembley loser with the
Blues a year earlier. In 1936, after eight
years' solid service and 226 appearances,
Matt Busby was sold to Liverpool for
£8,000 and played in one of the Anfield
club's best ever half-back lines with fellow Scots Bradshaw and McDougal. He
later became boss at Old Trafford,
moulding an exciting young team
together dubbed 'The Busby Babes'
before the team were involved in a tragic
air crash in Munich in February 1958.
Busby survived and guided United to
European Cup glory in 1968 before
retiring. He never forgot his Maine
Road roots, however, and had many
friends at City, Joe Mercer included.

BELOW Matt Busby in action

A MANCHESTER CITY A to Z | 19

Captains

BELOW Sam Cowan, 1926

BELOW Sam Cowan, 1926

MIDDLE Roy Paul clutches the FA Cup, 1956

FAR RIGHT Richard Dunne in action, 2006

CITY HAVE HAD SOME INSPIRA-tional leaders on the pitch over the years and Billy Meredith was the first captain to lift the FA Cup after a 1-0 win over Bolton Wanderers in 1904. Sam Cowan captained City to three FA Cup finals and Sam Barkas led the Blues to the 1946-47 Second Division title. One of the toughest and most determined skippers was Welsh central defender Roy Paul, who drove his side to success in the mid-Fifties on the threat of a clip on the nose if they didn't pull their weight! This was in evidence as City returned to pick up the FA Cup in 1956 after being beaten at the same stage a year earlier. Paul had vowed to take his team back and win the trophy the following season just as Sam Cowan had done 22 years earlier.

City's most successful captain was Tony Book. The influential, no-nonsense full-back captained the Blues to five trophies in four years, including

every domestic honour plus the European Cup Winners' Cup. Mike Doyle is the last captain to lift a knock-out trophy, skippering City to a 2-1 win against Newcastle in the 1976 League Cup final and Keith Curle wore the armband when the Blues achieved their highest finishes in Division One for 14 years – fifth – for two successive campaigns in 1991 and 1992. Andy Morrison cut a menacing figure in the centre of defence between 1998 and 2001 and he was inspirational as City escaped the Second Division at the first attempt in 1998-99. But for injury, his record would no doubt have been even more impressive.

Stuart Pearce's one season as skipper saw the side break many records and win the Second Division Championship in great style under his impeccable leadership. Algerian Ali Benarbia became a member of an exclusive band of foreign players to skipper City after taking the armband for the 2002-03 season and others include Bermudian striker Shaun Goater, Dutchman Gerard Wiekens and French defender Sylvain Distin. Irish centre-half Richard Dunne is the Blues' modern-day Captain Fantastic and has been at the club since 2000.

Celebrities

JOHNNY MARR, OASIS, Badly Drawn Boy, Doves, Rick Wakeman, Mike Pickering, Mark E Smith of The Fall and Take That's Jason Orange are all City fans, as was legendary Joy Division front man Ian Curtis. Olympic swimmer James Hickman, England rugby union stars Will Greenwood and Andy Farrell, world champion boxer Ricky Hatton, plus rugby league star Shaun Edwards all make for an impressive list of sporting fans.

ABOVE Take That's Jason Orange

ABOVE RIGHT Rick Wakeman

BELOW RIGHT Eddie Large

Stuart Hall, legendary presenter of 'It's a Knockout', is a lifelong City fan as is breakfast television presenter John Stapleton.

Roly-poly comedians Eddie Large and Bernard Manning have both followed the club since their childhood days, and Large was even a regular on the

City bench for a time during the 1980s. Soap stars Jeff Hordley, Bruce Jones, Sally Lyndsay, Amanda Barrie and Adam Rickett, are all City fans and David Threlfall – Frank Gallagher of Channel 4's Shameless, Craig Cash from BBC's The Royle Family, actor Warren Clarke and Hollywood actress Marsha Thomason also support City.

Championships

CITY HAVE WON TWO 'OLD' Division One Championships and had to wait until the last day of the season on each occasion – typical of the club! The historic first was in 1936-37 when an Eric Brook-inspired City beat Sheffield Wednesday 4-1 to clinch the trophy. In 1967-68 City travelled to Newcastle United, needing a win to ensure Manchester United and Liverpool could not overtake them on the final day. City won 4-3 and United had to settle for runners-up spot. The Blues have finished runners-up on three occasions, in 1903/04, 1920/21 and 1976/77.

There have been seven titles won in the old Division Two. The first was in 1898-99 and then four years later in 1902-03 and again in 1909-10 – the latter two following relegation the previous season. In 1927-28 City pipped Leeds United to the title by two points and in 1946-47 the Blues won the League by four points over Burnley and enjoyed a 22-match unbeaten run along the way. The 1965-66 title proved to be a prelude to the silverware-laden days of Mercer and Allison, and Kevin Keegan's entertaining City team were crowned the 'new' Division One in 2001/02, 10 points clear of West Bromwich Albion.

BELOW City celebrate winning the First Division Championship, 2002

City of Manchester Stadium

BELOW View of the match between England and Japan held at the City of Manchester Stadium, 2004

CITY MOVED INTO THEIR NEW state-of-the-art stadium in time for the start of the 2003/04 season. Christened the 'City of Manchester Stadium', it is widely regarded as one of the best in Britain and Europe. Housing 48,000 supporters, the futuristic design was also home to the hugely successful 2002 Commonwealth Games held in the city. Many believed the stadium should remain an athletics arena, but without City's commitment and financial backing, the new venue would, at best, have been a temporary sporting arena built and then dismantled afterwards. After the Games finished, the running track was dug up and the playing surface lowered several metres to uncover the lower tiers of each stand, which had been buried under tons of soil. A temporary stand was replaced in time for the Blues to take up permanent residence following 80 years at Maine Road. City opened the stadium by beating Barcelona 2-1 and the first competitive game was a UEFA Cup qualifier against Total Network Solutions that the Blues won 5-0. England have since played two friendlies at the stadium against Japan and Iceland, and the 2007/08 UEFA Cup final will be held there, too.

Colours

THINK SKY BLUE AND chances are you will think of the traditional home colours of Manchester City – unless you happen to be a Coventry fan, of course! But the colours don't go all the way back to the days when City were known as Gorton. They are believed to have worn black shirts with a large white cross on the front, which considering the club were founded as a church team, is wholly probable.

Ardwick FC wore mainly white but when they changed their name to Manchester City, the shift in shirt colours was to blue – Cambridge Blue at that – plus grey shorts. The shorts were ditched in 1896-97 in favour of white shorts with a plum-coloured change strip.

The favourite and what are believed to be the traditional colours of City – the light-blue shirts – didn't arrive until some years later. There have been numerous change strips in the past and most of them have been since the 1980s when a garish selection of colours and

designs were selected for the club's away kit, including luminous green and bright yellow. The red and black striped shirt from the late 1960s is a firm favourite with fans and is believed to have been the idea of Malcolm Allison who wanted City to resemble all-conquering Italians of the era, AC Milan. Suppliers of the kit have been Umbro, Kappa, Le Coq Sportif and Reebok.

ABOVE Robbie Fowler and Nicolas Anelka model the new home and away kits, 2003

Coppell

RIGHT Steve Coppell
meets the press, 1996

STEVE COPPELL'S 30-DAY stay as manager of Manchester City is the shortest reign on record and the brevity of the tenure is still something of a mystery today. The popular theory is that Coppell realised the position was too stressful and was making him ill. He later admitted that he knows the City fans must have been bemused by the whole situation but he just couldn't carry on. He was afforded a warm welcome by the fans, so whatever the problem was, it was off the pitch, one would assume, rather than on it. Considering Coppell's success in later years with other clubs, most notably Reading, it is a pity he couldn't see out the first few months and settle into the position as he is clearly a manager of some talent.

During his 30 days, City won twice, drew once and lost three times.

Corrigan

GOALKEEPER JOE CORRIGAN OR 'Big Joe', as he was affectionately known at Maine Road, played an astonishing number of times for the club – 592 in all – in a period stretching back 17 years. He signed as a junior from Sale FC and had to fight hard to establish himself as City's number one with the experienced duo of Ken Mulhearn and Harry Dowd ahead of him in the pecking order.

His early days were fraught with anguish and he was anything but a crowd favourite as he struggled with his form, confidence, and weight. His inconsistency led to him being transfer-listed in 1974, but Joe was determined to prove the doubters wrong. He buckled down, lost the excess pounds and improved to such an extent that he was called up to the England squad not long after and would surely have been the England first choice had he not been unfortunate enough to have had Peter Shilton and Ray Clemence in front of him.

The fans at Maine Road were in no

BELOW Joe Corrigan celebrates during the FA Cup semi-final against Ipswich Town, 1981

doubt about Corrigan's qualities and they voted him Player of the Year in 1976, 1978 and 1980 – a record number of awards.

With the emergence of Alex Williams and the lure of a fresh challenge overseas, he left City in 1983 to join Seattle Sounders in the USA, but returned to play for Brighton and Hove Albion not long after. On his return to Maine Road with the Seagulls, he was afforded a hero's welcome, with the fans giving him a standing ovation lasting several minutes. He won nine England caps in total but also played 10 times for the England 'B' team and represented his country at Under-21 and Under-23 levels. Joe now coaches at West Bromwich Albion. A braver goalkeeper would be hard to find.

Cowan

SAM COWAN JOINED CITY IN 1924 and served the club with great distinction for more than a decade. He captained the side in the 1933 FA Cup final after telling King George V that his team would be 'back next year to win it'. Sure enough, the Blues returned to win the trophy, just as he'd predicted and his place amongst the club's all-time greats was assured. He left City in 1935 and after playing for Bradford City and Brighton and Hove Albion, settled in Hove, East Sussex.

He became coach at Brighton and set up a successful physiotherapy practice near to the Seagulls' home ground in Hove. City asked if he would like to become the team manager in 1946 and Cowan, though still living near Brighton, accepted, but commuted to Manchester rather than return permanently. He guided the Blues to the Division Two Championship and looked set for a successful career in management, but his travelling meant the position became impossible for him and he decided he'd rather concentrate full time on his practice on the south coast. How successful Cowan might have been as a manager, one can only guess, but he was a born winner and losing him was a huge blow for the Blues.

FAR LEFT Joe Corrigan takes a breather

BELOW Sam Cowan (right), before the FA Cup, 1934

Cricketers

THERE HAVE BEEN TWO CITY players that were also first-class cricketers. 'Patsy' Hendren played 51 Test matches for England and scored over 40,000 runs for Middlesex. The well-built winger played only twice for the Blues during the 1908-09 season – clearly his chief talent was with the bat. Jack Dyson was a talented all-rounder for Lancashire scoring 4,433 runs and taking 161 wickets between 1954 and 1964. As one sporting season ended, the other began so holidays were a thing of fancy until his retirement from football.

He played 72 games for City (1951-61) in all competitions and scored 29 goals, including one in the 1956 FA Cup final. Continuing the theme, cricketers Andrew Flintoff, Matthew Maynard and Phil DeFreitas are all City fans.

Crossan

JOHNNY CROSSAN'S PATH TO Manchester City is quite a story in itself. Following irregularities in a transfer deal taking Johnny Crossan from Coleraine to Bristol City, the authorities slapped a sin die ban on the talented midfielder. He was left with no other choice but to seek a career on the continent and Sparta Rotterdam were suitably impressed after a trial and he was signed on by the Dutch side. He then moved on to Standard Liège in Belgium, playing in the European Cup during his time there. His skill and technique were taking on new dimensions and when the ban in the UK was lifted in 1962, Sunderland moved the quickest and snapped up the Northern Irish international for £28,000.

He proved a popular signing for the Roker Park faithful and that trend continued when Joe Mercer made him one of his first signings as City manager, paying £40,000 for his services. Mercer saw Crossan as the man who could help knit a talented young side together with his skill and experience. He was made captain, a role he revelled in, and City

won the Division Two Championship. Crossan's contribution was huge, missing just two League games all season and netting 13 goals.

Crossan was a hugely popular figure at Maine Road – skilful and feisty in the challenge, he had a heart as big as lion and didn't suffer fools gladly. After being involved in a car crash, he continued playing while hampered by a leg injury and told nobody at the club about his injury. Many mistook his laboured performances for laziness and some of the crowd showed their displeasure and a move away from the club became inevitable. At the end of the season Johnny Crossan was once again on the move, this time to Middlesbrough for £34,500.

Daley

STEVE DALEY JOINED City from Wolverhampton Wanderers for £1,437,500 in 1979 to become the most expensive British player ever. Malcolm Allison had reckoned the industrious Daley would be the perfect player to build his young side around, but it soon became clear that Daley was horribly out of his depth. Whether it was the weight of such a huge fee hanging around his neck or the weight of expectation that affected him, Daley never looked any better than a run-of-the-mill footballer at best. He soon became the focus of displeasure from fans that saw him as a waste of precious funds. He had looked a hard-working midfielder with ability at Molineux but the move to Maine Road sent his career spiralling into reverse. After 15 months of disappointment for all concerned, he signed for US club Seattle Sounders for a fraction of the fee paid for his services.

Derbies

THOUGH THE BLUES HAVE severely underperformed in the Manchester derby games over the past 20 years, it's still a fixture eagerly anticipated by both sets of fans. It's been almost 40 years since City dominated the fixture and during the late Sixties and early Seventies, City rarely lost a game against United. Favourite derby days include the 4-1 away win for City with Franny Lee notching a hat-trick and, in particular, the 1-0 win at Old Trafford in 1974 which rubber-stamped United's relegation to Division Two though few would have believed that would be the Blues' last win for more than three decades. Moving on 15 years, the 1989 5-1 win at Maine Road will never be forgotten by either sets of supporters with Mel Machin's young side ripping the Reds to shreds on a day when everything went right for the Blue half of Manchester. City enjoyed the first Manchester derby at the City of Manchester Stadium in 2004 when the Blues triumphed 4-1 and City also won 3-1 in 2006.

LEFT Richard Dunne pursues Wayne Rooney at Old Trafford, 2006

The complete record, up to the start of the 2007/08 season is:

League	Pld	W	D	L	F	A
City	137	35	48	54	181	199
United	137	54	48	35	199	181

FA Cup	Pld	W	D	L	F	A
City	7	2	0	5	5	9
United	7	5	0	2	9	5

League Cup	Pld	W	D	L	F	A
City	3	2	1	0	8	3
United	3	0	1	2	3	8

Totals:	Pld	W	D	L	F	A
City	147	39	49	59	194	211
United	147	59	49	39	211	194

RIGHT Keenly fought
Manchester derby, 1956

Deyna

THE 1978 WORLD CUP IN ARGENtina created much excitement in England, particularly when it was rumoured some of the top names in the tournament might be heading here. City fans were delighted to learn that the Blues were on the trail of 102-times capped Polish World Cup captain Kaziu Deyna, a massive star of Iron Curtain football. Red tape and the player's involvement in the Polish Army would initially delay the deal before a fee of £100,000 was agreed with Legia Warsaw. The Polish side asked City if they could pay the fee in the form of electronic goods such as copiers and fax machines, which they duly did. But though Deyna was undoubtedly a precocious talent, things never really ran smoothly during his time in Manchester. He was forced to look after his young son alone with his wife hospitalised in Poland for a lengthy period and it wasn't until he'd been with the club nine months at City that he finally found the back of the net.

Despite this, the technique, skill and vision Deyna possessed made him a huge favourite with the City faithful and

LEFT Kazimierz Deyna shortly after arriving at Maine Road, 1978

his first-season return of six goals in 11 starts promised even better to come for the following campaign. Beset by injuries and off-field problems, however, Deyna missed half of the campaign because of one reason or another and in January 1981, he left for San Diego in the NASL. Tragically, he was killed in a car crash in California in September 1989. His elegance and ability have ensured he is fondly remembered at Maine Road.

Dickov

CONSIDERING ALAN BALL DIDN'T personally sign Georgi Kinkladze, perhaps his most inspirational signing as City manager was Paul Dickov from Arsenal. Ball stayed just long enough to

see his best signing make his debut away to Stoke City in 1996 before being sacked by the Blues just three games into the 1996/97 campaign. Had Ball known sooner of the positive effect Dickov would have on his lacklustre side, he may well have signed him a year sooner. The £800,000 capture from Arsenal set about terrorising defenders from the word go and what he lacked in height and natural ability, he made up for in sheer guts and effort. He never really enjoyed the luxury of being an automatic first choice but his attitude did not waver and once he pulled on the laser-blue jersey the 5ft 5in pocket dynamo became like a man possessed, chasing lost causes and wearing down defenders both physically and mentally by never giving them a moment's peace.

Dickov's role in helping City recover from

the shock of finding themselves in mid-table in the nation's third division and heading for obscurity, to the Premiership within the space of 18 months, should never be underestimated and he was the catalyst that helped propel the Blues back to the top division.

It was Dickov's late equaliser in the play-off semi-final first leg with Wigan Athletic that ensured the Blues were on level pegging for the return games and, unforgettably, it was Dickov who changed the fate of City with a truly incredible last-gasp equaliser against Gillingham in the final that would eventually see the Blues win on penalties. He also sealed the promotion-clinching victory at Blackburn Rovers by scoring the final goal in a 4-1 win as City stormed back to the Premiership. Though his goals were crucial, his endeavour and attitude also helped earn many more points along the way. In a survey of Premiership defenders, both John Terry and Rio Ferdinand cited Dickov as one of their most difficult opponents.

He moved to Leicester in 2002 after failing to hold down a first-team spot under Kevin Keegan and later moved to

Blackburn Rovers. In 2006, he made an emotional return to the club in which he'd become part of folklore and once again, in a sky-blue jersey, began terrorising defenders.

Distin

RIGHT Peter Doherty

BELOW Distin playing in Hamburg, 2002

SYLVAIN DISTIN DESERVES HIS place among the very best defenders to have represented Manchester City. The tall Frenchman joined the Blues for a £4 million fee in June 2002 and in doing so became the club's most expensive defensive signing. Distin had spent much of the 2001/02 season on loan at Newcastle from Paris St Germain but when the Magpies dithered over a permanent deal, Kevin Keegan moved in with a firm bid and secured the services of one of France's best uncapped players. A quick, powerful player, at 6ft 4in, Distin is something of a man-mountain and has consistently been one of the club's best players. He skippered the side between 2003 and 2005 and formed a terrific partnership with Richard Dunne at the heart of the Blues' defence. Relatively injury-free during his time with City, his lung-bursting runs and energetic style make him one of the most exciting defenders in the Premiership, though when his contract expired in the summer of 2007, he opted to join Portsmouth on a free transfer.

Doherty

THE TREASURED IMAGE OF A MIL-lion cigarette cards and a true Roy of the Rovers type figure, Peter Doherty, old timers will tell you, was one of the greatest players ever to play for Manchester City. Though he was at Maine Road for a decade, seven of those years were during wartime and his 133 appearances amounted to a mere fraction of the amount he would have made had he played at almost any other time for the club.

Born in Magherafelt, Eire, the tall inside-forward became one of football's hottest properties while playing for Glentoran and it was City and Blackpool who put firm offers in and the Blues just edged the battle for his signature at a cost of £10,000 – then a club record. He soon became one of the legends of the game and was also a master tactician on the pitch. Doherty excelled at dribbling, tackling, passing and heading and had virtually every asset a player could wish for. He delighted the City fans with his endless energy. Doherty was the star

RIGHT Peter Doherty
playing in 1939

of the Championship-winning side of 1936/37, scoring 32 goals in 45 matches. Despite the success and talent of the team, City followed up the League title with relegation – despite having scored more goals than anybody else had managed! The outbreak of war meant no competitive football for seven years, though he still played 89 times, scoring 60 goals during wartime for the club. If those were added to his official total, he would have scored 141 goals in just 222 games. He occasionally turned out for other sides during the war and it was City's refusal to allow him to play for Derby in a cup match that made him quit the club almost as soon as the war ended. Peter died in April 1990 and a commemorative plaque was unveiled in his native Ireland several years ago.

Dunne

IF CITY HAD KNOWN JUST HOW much of an inspirational figure Richard Dunne would become for the club in future years, it's likely they would have paid triple the original £3.5m they shelled out to Everton in 2000. Quite simply, Dunne is one of the best defenders City have ever had.

Aged just 20, Dunne represented something of a gamble for manager Joe Royle and his early years at City suggested that gamble might not pay off. Though clearly talented, Dunne had a habit of shooting himself in the foot and was the subject of several breaches of club discipline, culminating in Kevin Keegan coming within an ace of sacking the player for one misdemeanour too many. Lurking beneath his jack-the-lad behaviour, however, was an unpolished diamond and Dunne gradually got his act together off the pitch to stunning effect on it. Deceptively quick and very skilful for a defender, he quickly won over the City supporters with a series of top-class defensive displays and he soon became viewed as irreplaceable and undoubtedly the club's most important

player. Since partnering Sylvain Distin, Dunne has earned a reputation of one of the best defenders in the Premiership, as important to City as John Terry is to Chelsea. The football equivalent of 'the immovable object', Dunne has been crowned Player of the Year for three successive years and took over the captain's armband in 2005. Loyal, totally committed and completely dependable – Dunne is a City legend in the making.

LEFT Richard Dunne battles for the ball with Alan Smith of Manchester United, 2007

England

COLIN BELL IS CITY'S LEADING cap winner for England with 48 and that figure would quite possibly have been almost doubled but for the devastating injury he sustained in 1975.

Centre-back Dave Watson earned 30 caps between 1975 and 1979 while Franny Lee won 27, also over a four-year period. Frank Swift won 19 caps and became only the second keeper to skipper England, while City record goal-scorer Eric Brook won just one less. Peter Barnes (14), Trevor Francis (10), Joe Corrigan (9), Mike Summerbee, Rodney Marsh and Ivor Broadis (8) all served their country proudly.

Other cap winners were: Bray, Tueart, Revie (6), Doyle and Barkas (5). Tilson, Burgess, Roberts and Royle each won four. Thirteen other City stars won three caps or less and the last of them to appear for the national team was Keith Curle, who won all three of his caps while being played out of position at full-back. Of the new batch of England stars, Shaun Wright-Phillips, Micah Richards and Joey Barton, all graduates of the club Academy, have all represented their country in recent years with Richards in particular looking the biggest threat to Bell's record in the coming years.

European Cup

CITY HAVE VENTURED INTO THE competition of European Champions –

when it was strictly for winners of the respective Leagues of Europe and not the cash cow the Champions League is today. Unfortunately, a mix of naivety and, on the part of coach Malcolm Allison, brash over-confidence, saw the Blues exit to far more experienced and wily opponents from the continent. Malcolm Allison's pre-match statement that his team would 'terrify Europe' didn't seem to help much either and fresh from being crowned League champions, City began the 1968-69 season full of hope and expecting to show Europe there were two teams in Manchester (United having won the tournament the previous season). Little was known about Turkish champions Fenerbahce when they ran out at Maine Road for the opening round's first leg, and the visitors proved to be master defensive tacticians, frustrating the hosts and the Maine Road fans during a 0-0 draw. The second leg, played in front of a hostile 45,000-crowd, looked to be tilting City's way when Tony Coleman scored a crucial away goal to open the scoring, but the home side rallied and eventually won 2-1. A tough lesson had been learned, but City would put it to good use just 12 months later…

FAR LEFT Manchester City and England goalkeeper Frank Swift making a save, 1948

MIDDLE Portrait of Dave Watson

LEFT Keith Curle of England in action during a European Championship match, 1992

European Cup Winners' Cup

A NOW DEFUNCT TOURNAMENT of Europe's domestic cup-winning sides this was one that Manchester City mastered and almost success-fully defended. The FA Cup final victory over Leicester City had given Joe Mercer's side a fast-track back into Europe following the European Cup disappointment 12 months earlier. In what would prove to be an exciting adventure on the continent, the Blues put on a terrific display of gutsy, attacking football to hold Atletico Bilbao to a 3-3 draw in Spain and then dispatched them confidently 3-0 at Maine Road. Belgian side SK Lierse were soundly beaten 3-0 on their own soil and then 5-0 in Manchester. The Blues were playing their own brand of exhilarating football and it was sweeping aside all-comers. But they'd learned a lesson against Fenerbahce and when they faced defensive opposition in the form of Academica Coimbra, City patiently

played out a tactical game of chess, drawing 0-0 in Portugal and

side Schalke 04, losing the away leg 1-0 but running riot at Maine Road and winning 5-1. At last, Allison's prediction that City would be the enfant terrible of European football had become reality.

Goals from Franny Lee and Neil Young helped City beat Polish side Gornik Zabrze in the final, played in atrocious conditions in the Prater Stadium, Vienna. City had their first – and to date only – European trophy. In defence of the ECWC, only an injury crisis at a critical stage denied City the chance of another appearance in the final after the Blues successfully saw off the challenges of Linfield, Honved and Gornik Zabrze to reach the semi-finals for the second successive year. Pitted against Chelsea, the only other English team left, and with a crippling injury list including Alan Oakes, Colin Bell, Mike Doyle, Glyn Pardoe and Mike Summerbee, City lost both legs by a single goal. With a fit and full squad, Mercer's side may well have gone on to win the Cup Winners' Cup again.

edging the second leg 1-0. City moved into the semi-finals to face German

FA Cup – triumphs

WINNERS ON FOUR OCCASIONS and finalists on another four visits to Wembley, City have done fairly well in the FA Cup over the past 112 years. The first time the Blues lifted the trophy was in 1904 with a narrow 1-0 win over Bolton at The Crystal Palace; the same season they missed out on a historic league and cup double after finishing runners-up in Division One. Bolton would have their revenge in 1926, winning the cup by scoring the game's only goal in City's first-ever Wembley appearance. Seven years after that, City were again on the losing side, this time to Everton by a crushing scoreline of 3-0. Captain Sam Cowan vowed to return with his side the following year and lift the trophy as winners, and he was true to word as the Blues beat Portsmouth 2-1 in the 1934 final.

History repeated itself in 1955 when City went down 3-1 to Newcastle United only to go all the way the next year and win the competition 3-1 over Birmingham City. It would be 1969 before the Blues tasted more success in the world's most famous club competitions – a Neil Young thunderbolt giving Joe Mercer's side a 1-0 victory over Leicester. The last appearance in the final by City was in 1981 when Tottenham triumphed 3-2 in a replay, the first match ending 1-1. There were memorable goals by Tommy Hutchison, Steve Mackenzie and Ricky Villa over the two matches, watched by a combined attendance of 192,500.

FA Cup – shocks

IT'S AN UNFORTUNATE FACT OF life that the Blues have become a sizeable scalp to numerous lower league opponents over the years with the third-round defeat at Fourth Division Halifax Town in 1980 arguably the most embarrassing. The Blues, managed by Malcolm Allison, ran out to the shambolic surrounds of The Shay, replete with a 70-year-old roof from former City home ground Hyde Road and contested the game on a glue-pot of a pitch. With record-signing Steve

Daley, probably worth more than the entire Halifax team, failing to inspire City, the game looked to be heading for a 0-0 draw. Then, with 10 minutes to go, Halifax striker Paul Hendrie tucked away a low drive that proved to be the winner. Malcolm Allison later claimed the stain of the result would never be wiped clean. He was right and the game is replayed on third-round day year after year as TV companies harp on about the 'romance' of the competition. The year before, City had gone down 2-0 to Third Division Shrewsbury Town, on a rock-solid frosty pitch at Gay Meadow that many believe should never have been played and further embarrassments included a 2-1 defeat at Blackpool in 1984, a 3-1 loss to Brentford in 1989 and a 1-0 reverse at Cardiff City in 1994.

RIGHT Let there be light

Floodlights

'LET THERE BE LIGHT' – AND there was – and midweek evening games became an atmospheric new addition to the English league season. Four towering floodlights were erected at Maine Road in 1953 and the inaugural floodlit match was a friendly against Hearts on 14 October that same year. The Blues wore special 'shiny shirts' for the evening and won an entertaining game 6-3 in front of almost 24,000 curious fans. The innovative lighting brought Manchester United back to Maine Road (they had ground shared with City during the Second World War) to play various friendlies and cup games until Old Trafford had their own installed in 1957. Not, however, before Maine Road became the first English ground to play host to a European Cup match in 1956 – though sadly the Blues weren't even involved as United beat RSC Anderlecht 10-0.

Foe

FEW COULD HAVE REALISED THE long-lasting impression Marc Vivien Foe would leave on Manchester City fans following his season-long loan deal from French side Lyon. A holding midfielder, the tall Cameroonian was signed by Kevin Keegan to add steel to a creative midfield that included Eyal Berkovic, Ali Benarbia and Shaun Wright-Phillips and though initially he wasn't appreciated by the majority of City fans, it soon became clear that he was doing a fantastic job for the team, not dissimilar to the role Patrick Vieira had done so effectively for Arsenal for several years. Foe then added several vital goals to the City cause, with his telescopic legs connecting to several half-chances and his popularity soared. During the penultimate game to be played at Maine Road, City took on Sunderland and it was Foe who scored what turned out to be the last goal by a City player at the famous old stadium in a 3-0 win. At the end of the 2002/03 season, Keegan began negotiations to bring Marc Vivien to City on a permanent basis, but during a

Confederations Cup match for Cameroon against Colombia in June 2003, he slumped to the floor having suffered a massive and fatal heart attack. He was just 28 years old. The shockwaves were felt throughout the sporting world and the now closed Maine Road became a shrine of flowers, shirts and scarves from all around the world as fans paid their respects to this most gentle, popular man.

Football League Cup

KNOWN ALSO AS THE MILK CUP, Rumbelows Cup, Littlewoods Cup, Coca-Cola Cup, Worthington Cup and more lately, the Carling Cup, the League Cup has always played second fiddle to the FA Cup. The trophy came into existence in 1960 and City's first match was a 3-0 win over Stockport County. Four years later and Stoke City defeated the Blues over two legs in the semi-final by an aggregate of 2-1. Happier times were

ahead, however, and in 1970, the cup finally found its way to the Maine Road. Victories over Southport, Liverpool, Everton and QPR set up a semi-final with Manchester United over two legs. City won 2-1 at Maine Road, but trailed by the same score in the return leg with just a few minutes left on the clock. City then won an indirect free-kick on the edge of the United box and Franny Lee took a crack at goal. Alex Stepney could have stepped aside and the goal wouldn't have counted but instead he parried the thunderous drive to Mike Summerbee, who tucked away the equaliser. In the final, City slugged it out against West Bromwich Albion on a glue-pot of a pitch and it took an extra-time winner from Glyn Pardoe to settle affairs by a score of 2-1.

City returned in 1974 under Ron Saunders but lost 2-1 to Wolves with Colin Bell the scorer. Two years later and City dispatched Norwich City, Nottingham Forest, Manchester United,

Mansfield Town and Middlesbrough to earn the right to play Newcastle United at Wembley. Peter Barnes opened the scoring before Alan Gowling levelled for the Magpies, but Dennis Tueart's spectacular overhead goal won the game 2-1 for the Blues.

The last time City made a real impression on the League Cup was in 1980-81 when John Bond's side met Liverpool in the last four, losing 2-1 on aggregate over two legs.

ABOVE Happy players and officials after a 2-1 victory in the football League Cup final, 1976

Francis

MORE THAN 10,000 CITY FANS travelled to Stoke to watch Trevor Francis make his debut for the Blues after the much-coveted striker joined the club in 1981 for £1.2m. The England man didn't disappoint, either, scoring twice in a 3-1 win. Francis positively oozed class and he was graceful and electrifying to watch. His stay at Maine Road, however, was blighted by injury, though he inspired City to top the table over the 1981 festive period following a 3-1 Boxing Day victory at Liverpool and a 2-1 win against Wolves, two days later. He only managed 29 appearances for the Blues but scored 14 goals including several fantastic individual efforts. An intelligent forward, he would bring others into the game and inspired those around him, especially the younger forwards, to reach greater heights but the stop/start nature of his time at the club proved frustrating to everyone, not least the player. He reluctantly joined Italian Serie A club Sampdoria for approximately £1 million having played for just one season at Maine Road – the truth was the cash-strapped Blues could no longer afford to keep their prized asset, though the impression he'd left was huge.

Full Members' Cup

THIS MUCH-MALIGNED COMPETI-
tion was sponsored by several obscure
companies during its relatively brief
existence. The Simod Cup, Zenith Data
Systems... call it what you will, but it
was the plain old Full Members' Cup in
1985/86 when City first tentatively
entered and it would be the one and
only occasion the trophy registered in
the hearts and minds of the Blues' support. With English clubs banned from
European competition, the FMC hoped
to become the third major cup competition in England, but it was always
destined to fail due to lack of prestige
and no real incentive to win the trophy.
Considered as little more than a joke by
most of the football world, both City
and Chelsea progressed through the
rounds in front of sparse crowds, until
they met at Wembley. Despite the
general apathy surrounding the competition, some 68,000 fans turned out on
the day and enjoyed a quite spectacular
feast of attacking football that ebbed
and flowed in the dramatic traditions
befitting both clubs. City went ahead
through Mark Lillis but the Pensioners
roared back with vengeance to lead 5-1
with just minutes left. Incredibly, City
pulled back three goals through Lillis,
Kinsey and an own goal, and almost
scrambled an equaliser, ultimately
losing 5-4. The Blues never again
reached such dizzy heights in the
competition and their last appearance
was in 1991-92. The competition ceased
completely a couple of years later.

BELOW Mark Lillis celebrates his goal, 1985/86 Full Members' Cup Final

Gibson

RIGHT Maine Road was the best playing surface in the country

STAN GIBSON, HEAD groundsman at Maine Road since August 1960, passed away at his home close to Maine Road on Christmas Eve, 2001 aged 76 years old. An almost legendary figure at Maine Road, Stan was one of the finest groundsmen that this country has ever produced. He was approached by a whole host of clubs including Manchester United and most notably by England, who all tried to tempt him to tend their pitches with the same loving care he did at Maine Road by offering him bigger wages. They were wasting their time. Stan had blue blood running through his veins and was totally committed to making Maine Road into the best playing surface in the country – a feat he managed comfortably, year after year. The pitch regularly resembled a bowling green with its lush, green velvety surface and that gave the club the chance to play the passing, attractive style of football the supporters demanded. Club secretary Bernard Halford once said: 'Stan could grow grass on concrete' – and he probably did. Maine Road was never the same again without Stan.

Goater

SHAUN GOATER – OR 'THE GOAT' as he became almost universally known and loved – managed to turn jeers of derision into flat-out hero worship over a six-year period at Maine Road. Signed by Joe Royle for a bargain £400,000 from Bristol City, few regarded him as little more than a stop-gap – a journeyman striker whose goals might save the club from relegation to the Third Division in 1997/98. His four goals in nine starts weren't enough and he found himself playing for a side who'd been replaced in a higher division by his old side – Bristol City having won promotion. Goater's unorthodox style certainly got results, but it would be almost two years before the fans realised his hard work and honest style were actually a refreshing change to many of the game's over-pampered stars, and an appreciation quickly grew. It was also the first time in many, many years that the Blues had an instinctive striker who could bang in 20 to 30 goals without fail each season. Shaun's goals steered City out of Division Two in 1999 and his 29 goals the following campaign ensured a second successive promotion for the Blues. Injury beset the Bermudian international during the doomed 2000/01 Premiership campaign, but he still finished the season in red-hot form with seven in his last nine games, proving he could score goals anywhere, and his 32 goals in 2001/02 enabled the Blues to win promotion back to the Premiership at the first attempt. In his final season, he scored his 100th goal for the club in the historic final Manchester derby at Maine Road and his anthem, 'Feed the Goat and he will score', became one of the most famous football chants in football.

Grounds

ENCOMPASSING ALL THE NAMES City have played under, the following is a list of the grounds the club has, at some point or other, called home:

1880-81	Clowes Street
1881-82	Kirkmanshulme Lane Cricket Club
1882-84	Queens Road
1884-85	Pink Bank Lane
1885-87	The Bull's Head Hotel, Reddish Lane
1887-1923	Hyde Road
1923-2003	Maine Road
2003–	City of Manchester Stadium

RIGHT Maine Road, 1995

Hartford

SCOTTISH INTERNATIONAL ASA Hartford must have had one of the most famous medicals in the history of football after a hole was discovered in his heart on the eve of a move from West Brom to Leeds United. Crestfallen, Hartford continued to ply his trade at the Hawthorns before City boss Tony Book made an offer for his services and, after a stringent medical, he was given the green light by the doctor who said the condition should have no bearing whatsoever on his football career. A busy, all-action midfielder, Hartford was signed from West Brom in 1974 for a fee of £250,000 and he soon became the beating heart of the 1970s City team. Asa went on to win 36 caps for his country while at Maine Road – a record number of Scottish caps for a City player – and formed an excellent partnership with Gary Owen and Peter Barnes.

He was the driving force behind the Blues' bid to lift the League title in 1976-77 when they agonisingly missed out by a point to Liverpool. He was sold by Malcolm Allison in 1979 to Nottingham Forest for £500,000, but returned to City two years later, making another 88 appearances before jetting off for the North American Soccer League. He returned to the club for a third spell in 1995 to assist Alan Ball after management spells at Shrewsbury and Stockport and later took charge of the reserves until 2006.

ABOVE Asa Hartford, 1978

Hayes

BUT FOR A SERIOUS KNEE injury, Kearsley-born striker Joe Hayes would probably have been City's all-time top goalscorer. As it was, he fell just 26 short of Eric Brook's record of 178 having bagged 152 goals in 363 games. Hayes was a poacher supreme and scored one of the goals in the 1956 FA Cup final victory over Birmingham City. A pocket dynamo, legend has it that he arrived for a trial game at Maine Road with his boots in a brown-paper parcel and duly scored four goals. Two months later, he made his debut against Tottenham Hotspur aged only 17. He played alongside the likes of Dave Ewing, Bobby Johnstone, Johnny Hart, Don Revie and Joe Fagan. Hayes' only international honours were two England Under-23 caps – scant reward for a striker with such a prolific record. Joe had worked in a cotton mill and a colliery before signing for the Blues so it wasn't difficult for him to keep his feet on the ground at a huge club like City. At 5ft 8in, he wasn't the tallest of forwards and he also had poor eyesight, but Joe Hayes made the very best of his abilities and still sits proudly among the top all-time scorers for the Blues more than four decades on.

Heslop

VERSATILITY WAS THE NAME OF the game for defender George Heslop, who joined City from Everton in 1965 for £20,000. Joe Mercer moved in for him after he'd failed to establish himself at either Goodison Park or his previous club, Newcastle United where each time he'd been in the shadow of legendary centre-halves who were rarely injured. Under Mercer, however, Heslop finally gained the first-team berth that had eluded him elsewhere. His contribution during City's historic trophy-winning period was immense and, in his first four years at Maine Road, Heslop had collected four medals for winning the Second Division, First Division, League Cup and European Cup Winners' Cup. Perhaps now past his peak, Heslop's remaining years at City were spent between the first team and the reserves, and in 1971 he joined Cape Town City on loan for a year before eventually joining Bury for £3,000. He later went on to become licensee at the Hyde Road Hotel – the original headquarters of Manchester City Football Club, though later moved into the social services sector. He sadly passed away in 2006.

BELOW George Heslop (left), holds onto Chelsea's centre-forward Peter Osgood during a tackle, 1971

Horne

RIGHT Stan Horne, 1967

HALF-BACK STAN HORNE DESERVES his place in history as much as any Manchester City player down the years. Though perhaps a lesser-known figure than some of the more illustrious names to have represented the Blues, Horne never let the club down during his four years at Maine Road and was part of the squad that won the Division Two and Division One titles within the space of three years. Injury robbed Stan of a greater career at Maine Road and it was his misfortune to have had so many top-quality players around him that made it all but impossible to win back his place by the time he'd returned to full fitness. Stan followed manager Joe Mercer from Aston Villa after a misdiagnosed blood pressure condition had threatened his career. He was preparing for medical retirement but on a whim decided to write to his former boss Mercer at City and ask for the chance of proving himself fit. Joe granted him a trial, was impressed by what he saw and gave him a contract.

After establishing himself in the team, Stan suffered a crippling snapped

Achilles' tendon and was out for the rest of the year, and by the time he returned, the Blues were assembling a side that would take on – and invariably beat – the best teams in the country. With the likes of Mike Doyle, Alan Oakes and George Heslop now well ahead of him in the queue for a first-team place, he realised it was time to move on.

He made 63 starts plus three more as substitute and was the very first black player to sign and play for the Blues.

Hutchison

TOMMY HUTCHISON'S TIME AS A Manchester City player was relatively brief in the grand scheme of things and his 57 starts bear testament to that. But the stylish Scottish winger oozed class and left a long-lasting impression on those Blues fans that were fortunate enough to see him play. He joined City from Coventry for just £47,000 and formed part of John Bond's famous 'tartan trio' that also included Gerry Gow and Bobby McDonald. Together, they helped transform an ailing City side into a team that almost won the 1981 FA Cup. Hutchison possessed excellent control and vision and a will to play football the way it was meant to be played. Due to his unfortunate and unique record, Tommy has the dubious privilege of appearing on a Trivial Pursuit question card. The question is: who is the only player to score for both sides in an FA Cup final? Of course, the answer is Tommy Hutchison, who scored with a flying header for City in the first half and then deflected home a Spurs free-kick after eavesdropping on Glenn Hoddle's plans.

BELOW Tommy Hutchison scoring the opening goal of the 100th FA Cup Final against Spurs, 1981

Hyde Road

NOW THE SITE OF A MANCHESTER bus company, Hyde Road was City's first enclosed ground and was home to Ardwick FC from 1887 to 1894 and then Manchester City FC from 1894 until 1923. Hemmed in by a railway track to the west and north sidings – train drivers would often slow down to catch a glimpse of City in action, presumably giving a toot on their whistle if things appeared to be going well. Crowds were only estimated at the time and gates ranged from as low as 500 up to 40,000. The Blues were Division One runners-up on two occasions while at the ground, but with the team's popularity growing at a phenomenal rate, it became clear that a new home was desperately needed. Even more so after the Main Stand burned down in 1920. Belle Vue, a few miles up the road, was cited as a possible home, but the eight-acre plot was not nearly enough to house the club. Suitable land was found in Moss Side, several miles away, and the foundations of a new stadium were soon visible to curious supporters. In the summer of 1923, Maine Road was completed and City closed the gates at Hyde Road for the last time. One of the Hyde Road stands was sold to Halifax Town for the princely sum of £1,000 and was still standing when the Blues lost 1-0 at The Shay in 1980. Today, the area the pitch once occupied is now a skid pan for training bus drivers!

RIGHT Niall Quinn in action

FAR RIGHT Stephen Ireland, 2006

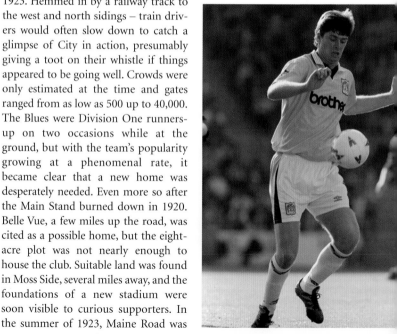

Ireland

CITY HAVE HAD STRONG connections to Ireland for many years with many Kippax favourites emanating from the Emerald Isle over the years. Peter Doherty was one of the greatest players to cross the water and play for the Blues but Niall Quinn won the most caps while at City. Richard Dunne looks certain to pass Quinn's tally of 38 and Stephen Ireland broke into the Irish side while still a teenager and scored three goals in his first four appearances for his country. Mick McCarthy played for Ireland while at City and, of course, he went on to manage the national side.

Johnson

Tommy Johnson in England strip, 1932

WITH 38 LEAGUE GOALS IN ONE season, Tommy Johnson is likely to retain his record of most strikes in one campaign for many, many years to come. He is second only to winger Eric Brook in the list of all-time goal-scorers for the club, but he may never have had the chance of such enduring fame but for City defender Eli Fletcher, who insisted the club sign the promising youngster from Dalton Casuals. In fact, so adamant was Fletcher that he threatened to leave the Blues unless they made Johnson a City player – Fletcher might unwittingly have been one of the first football agents of his day!

Fortunately, the club heeded the advice – or veiled threats – and Johnson, nicknamed 'Boy' because of his youthful appearance, marked his debut in 1919 with a goal but would take three more years to establish himself fully in the Blues' starting line-up. He formed an impressive partnership with Horace Barnes and also won two international caps for England while at City. The hugely popular striker finally moved on to Everton in 1930 for £6,000, much to the supporters chagrin and ironically played a large part in the 1933 FA Cup final win for the Toffees over the City. What Eli Fletcher made of it all is unknown...

LEFT Bobby Johnstone, 1955

Johnstone

BOBBY JOHNSTONE EARNED THE nickname 'Bobby Dazzler' for his exceptional skill on the ball. Born in Selkirk, the Scottish international arrived at Maine Road in March 1955 from Hibernian for a fee of £20,700. He made a sensational start to his Scotland career when he scored against England at Wembley, establishing him as one of the hottest properties of his generation. He quickly became a popular figure on the terraces, too, with his attacking instincts and ability, striking the right chords with the Blues' supporters. He made his debut against Bolton Wanderers and quickly made his way into the history books, when he became the first player ever to score in consecutive FA Cup finals in 1955 and 1956. In all, he played 138 times for City, winning four of his 17 Scotland caps while at Maine Road, and rifled in 50 goals before he was transferred back to Hibs for £7,000 in 1959. He was also a keen cricketer and crown green bowler and finished his career playing for Oldham Athletic. Bobby died in 2001, aged 71.

Keegan

FEW MANAGERS COULD LAY CLAIM to such an electrifying first season as the one enjoyed by Kevin Keegan in 2001/02. The former England legend was installed at Maine Road following Joe Royle's surprise sacking in May 2001 and his first signings were Stuart Pearce and Eyal Berkovic. His first game in charge against Watford was a fantastic occasion, as the City fans packed Maine Road hoping to be entertained by the man who made Newcastle United into one of the most attractive teams of the 1990s, and went home delighted by what they'd seen. 'The Keegan Factor', as it became known, encouraged open, attacking football and when he added Algerian midfielder Ali Benarbia into the mix, the football became a sublime fusion of devastating offensive play and something close to exhibition football. The fans lapped it up and City won the

First Division at a canter, breaking a host of records along the way, not least goals scored which totalled 108 in the league alone. As the Blues rolled back into the Premiership, so a galaxy of expensive talents was assembled at Maine Road, including the likes of Nicolas Anelka, Sylvain Distin and Peter Schmeichel. The Blues finished ninth in the Premiership and qualified for Europe via the Fair Play League. Nothing, it seemed could go wrong. More big names arrived in the form of David Seaman, Robbie Fowler and Steve McManaman but the team had lost much of its zip and invention with Benarbia and Berkovic gone and not adequately replaced. A brush with relegation during the Blues' first season at the City of Manchester Stadium in 2003/04 and a disappointing 2004/05 campaign saw Keegan quit City, seemingly having lost the ability to motivate his players. Stuart Pearce, Keegan's recently appointed coach took the reins and the man they called 'Mighty

Mouse' disappeared into the ether. For the first two years, however, Keegan was simply 'King Kev' to the goal-hungry City fans.

Kidd

DESPITE A FAIRLY SLOW START IN front of goal, it didn't take too long for Brian Kidd to erase the memory of his heroics for Manchester United following a £110,000 buy from Arsenal in 1976. 'Kiddo' would play a large part in

City's successful mid-1970s team and he seemed to enjoy ruffling the feathers of one or two former team-mates during the Manchester derby games. He took 10 games in the League to find the net for the new club and by the end of November he'd managed just one strike in 13 games. But if there were any doubters, they were well and truly silenced as Kidd suddenly hit form – and then some. He scored 10 goals in his next seven outings and struck four times in a 5-0 win over Leicester City, finishing the season with 21 goals from 39 games – his efforts had almost helped bring home the Championship in his first season.

City finished fourth a year on and Kidd impressed again with 16 goals from 39 league games. He also won the goal of the month on BBC 1's Match of the Day for the superb diving header he scored against Aston Villa on New Year's Eve 1977. The 1978-79 season started with Kidd scoring in all the first three games but just four more in his next 16 starts for the Blues signalled the end of his time with the blue half of the city as he joined Everton in March 1979 for £150,000.

Kinkladze

LITTLE WAS KNOWN OF 21-YEAR-old midfielder Georgi Kinkladze when he signed for City shortly before the start of the 1995/96 campaign. New manager Alan Ball took just one training session to claim that the Georgian would have the City fans 'hanging from the rafters to watch him play'.

Not long into his debut against Spurs on a hot, sunny August afternoon, it was clear to all in attendance that Kinkladze had the kind of individual skill rarely – if ever – seen at Maine Road before. Within a few months he was idolised by the fans and heralded by the pundits and the national media. He was a precocious talent – someone who got people out of their seats with his incredible dribbles and incisive precision passing. He made goals, scored them and invariably there would be at least two or three moments in a game when he could take your breath away.

Each goal he scored for the club was memorable and the solo effort against Southampton when he beat five players before chipping the ball impudently past Dave Beasant is regarded by most

RIGHT
Georgi Kinkladze, 1997

FAR RIGHT
The Kippax Stand,
Maine Road

as the best ever goal by a Manchester City player. 'Kinky', however, couldn't stop the Blues escaping relegation when a 2-2 draw with Liverpool was not enough to prevent City returning to Division One.

It wasn't long before Liverpool and Barcelona were linked with £10 million swoops for the player fans knew simply as 'Kinky' and Sir Alex Ferguson, off record, is alleged to have said that the only player at that time he would have signed was Kinkladze, but he knew City would never sell their prized asset to their most deadly rivals.

Gio stayed to try and help the Blues bounce back at the first attempt, sparkling here and there and scoring a dozen league goals along the way. City finished a disastrous 14th, but following an amazing show of support for the Georgian in the final game of the season at home to Reading, he decided to give it one last shot.

His final year was not a happy one. He looked frustrated and disappointed as City headed towards Division Two. Frank Clark had taken over from Ball and Joe Royle took over from Clark as the managerial merry-go-round continued at the club. Royle was bemused by what he felt was an unhealthy obsession with Kinky at the club and sold him to Ajax not long after arriving. The love affair between the City fans and Kinky was over. The memories of this most gifted player, at his very best, will last for many years.

Kippax Stand

HOME TO THOUSANDS UPON thousands of City fans since 1923, this famous, much-loved old terrace was often the extra man for the Blues as the supporters roared their heroes on to success. It could also mean the end of a player if the poor soul wasn't performing well over a period of time with many an opposing winger turning a pasty shade of white at the sight of a packed Kippax terrace.

It was over 35 years before a roof was erected to keep the incessant rain off the supporters' heads and, with a smart new covering, the side of the ground known generally as the 'popular side' was officially named the Kippax Stand. It was home to 32,000 fans, though this was reduced to 26,155 when the North Stand was completed in 1971. Further reductions meant that only 18,300 City fans stood in the cavernous old stand near its lamentable demise.

The Taylor Report, a government-backed investigation into the safety of standing areas at football grounds, recommended that all terracing become seated areas, effectively signalling the

end for the Kippax as a terraced stand. City supporters paid their final respects to their favourite part of the ground on 30 April 1994 when City took on Chelsea. Fancy dress, flags and balloons festooned the Kippax and celebrated its 71-year life. Many shed a tear after the final whistle and attempted to chip bits of concrete off steps as a souvenir.

The new Kippax stand was opened to City fans for the first home game of the 1995-96 season and many fans groaned as they took their seats in the second and the top tiers on first inspection – nothing to do with the perfect view of the pitch, but because Old Trafford was now visible in the distance!

Lake

PAUL LAKE IS THE GREATEST player City almost had. Destined for legendary status, Lake was tipped to be the new Colin Bell and, but for injury, he may well have scaled the heights of Bell, who ironically also saw his career cruelly robbed of several years. Such was Lake's abundant quality, he was deployed in a variety of positions for the Blues with equal aplomb. Full-back, centre-half or central midfield – Lake could play anywhere and make it look like his natural role. Predicted to be a future England skipper, Lake progressed through the club's youth system and was on the verge of a full call-up to the England squad when the first major injury setback struck. Lake was beset by injury and suffered more than any footballer should have to in his career. His attempt to overcome devastating knee ligament damage was both brave and, ultimately, destined to fail.

A harmless-looking fall in a home game with Aston Villa would rule Lake out for two years. His comeback in the 1992-93 season lasted two matches. He'd rushed his comeback knowing his knee wasn't quite right and his old injury resurfaced for what would tragically be the last game of his career. Despite several 'revolutionary' new operations, Lake retired from the game and moved into physiotherapy. Such was the respect for the player, more than 25,000 turned up for his testimonial against United on the same day his wife gave birth to their first child.

ABOVE Paul Lake, 1989

LEFT Ian Bishop and Paul Lake celebrate victory against Manchester United, 1989

RIGHT Portrait of
Denis Law, 1960

Law

THOUGH LAW SPENT THE BEST years of his career at Old Trafford, he had enough memorable games in a City shirt – over two spells separated by a decade – to be forgiven for his efforts elsewhere. One of the game's most instinctive strikers, he once famously scored a double hat-trick against Luton, only for the game to be abandoned due to the torrential rain creating a surface more suitable for canoeing than football. Typically, City lost the re-match 3-1 and Law had to be content with a consolation goal.

Joining City from Huddersfield Town, the scrawny teenage Law scored 23 times in his first season at Maine Road (29 times if you throw in the abandoned match) before Italian giants Torino made a British record offer of £125,000 which City accepted. As time went on, the talented Scot found his way to what would become his spiritual home with the Reds before returning to Maine Road for one last hurrah, having been released by United. Even in the twilight of his career, Law scored important goals for the Blues and featured in a dream – though ageing – forward line of Marsh, Summerbee and Lee. His final kick in League football was an impish back-heel that confirmed his former club United's relegation to Division Two. How they must have regretted allowing such a lethal talent to join their deadly rivals.

Lee

A PLAYER WHO CAN TRULY BE called a Manchester City legend, Francis Lee signed for City in 1967 aged 23, and was destined to become one of Joe Mercer's most influential signings. The Blues paid £60,000 for the stocky forward's services and for many, he was the final piece of the jigsaw that Mercer and Allison had put together. A lethal finisher, with a cannonball shot, Franny was also the most prolific penalty taker the club has ever known with many arguing he won spot-kicks unfairly. His

15 penalties in one season is easily a club record and he earned the nickname 'Lee One Pen'. He averaged just under a goal every other game for City and was an integral member of City's glory days, forging a fantastic understanding with Mike Summerbee and Colin Bell, dubbed 'The Holy Trinity'. A feisty so and so in a team of feisty so and sos, Lee was a born winner and he simply would not accept defeat. His exploits for City are legendary but there was a sour end to his time at Maine Road and in 1974 when he wasn't offered the kind of financial package he believed he was worth, he was allowed to join Derby

LEFT Francis Lee getting down to grass roots

County. Still angry at City's decision to sell him after all he had achieved for the club, he inspired Derby to the league title in his first year at the Baseball Ground and scored a blistering goal on his return to Maine Road just for good measure causing Match of the Day commentator Barry Davies to famously cry

'Look at his face! Just look at his face!'

He eventually did return to City but this time as chairman. He promised much and had been the saviour of fans eager to see Peter Swales step down after many trophy-less years. The takeover battle was bitter and drawn out, but fan-power won the day and Lee was installed in his new role. The millions of pounds that were promised to buy new players never really materialised and his first appointment as manager was Alan Ball – a move that left many supporters disappointed. Unfortunately, it was a pointer to Lee's reign as chairman and he never quite delivered the goods for the fans who had helped him into power. In 1998, barely four years into his tenure, Lee was – ironically – forced to step down by fan pressure. Considering his achievements, it is, with hindsight, a pity things turned out the way they did, though nobody can take away his achievements as a player and perhaps his spell as chairman was, if nothing else, well intentioned.

RIGHT Francis Lee in a match against Crystal Palace, 1972

Maine Road

HOME TO MANCHESTER CITY Football Club from 1923 until 2003, the club finally ended its 80-year tenure at the famous old ground for the last time against Southampton on 11 May 2003. City first played at their new home in 1923, just four months after Wembley Stadium was completed, having left behind Hyde Road and its limited capacity. Designed by local architect Charles Swain, the original plan was for the ground to match Wembley and hold 90,000 spectators – 'a stadium fit for Manchester's premier club' – as stated by officials at the time.

The opening game in August 1923 was greeted with great enthusiasm by the club's legions of fans, many of whom were in awe of its size. With only the Main Stand's 10,000 seats covered, the rest of the ground was open terracing, but buoyed on by a record crowd of

56,993, the Blues beat Sheffield United 2-1 with goals from Tom Johnson and

Second Division champions. Maine Road has seen various changes over the years but was undoubtedly most famous for its huge terrace, the Kippax, where most City fans gathered on match days. The various stands – the North Stand (formerly the Scoreboard End), Platt Lane and the Main Stand (and later, the new Kippax Stand) – were all developed at different stages over a number of years, giving the stadium an unusual, patched-together look.

None of the four roofs matched but that, to the supporters, was part of its appeal and in many ways Maine Road's eccentric look matched the team's eccentric play over the 80 years the club resided there. Shortly after the gates were locked for the final time in 2003, Maine Road was razed to the ground along with thousands of memories – happy, sad, bittersweet and joyous. Gone, but never forgotten, Maine Road will remain in City fans' hearts for many years to come.

Horace Barnes. The next home game proved that the new ground was sadly not impregnable and City lost 2-1 to Aston Villa but the club would lose just twice more at home that season.

The 'popular side', later known as the Kippax, had a flagpole positioned roughly level with the halfway line at the very back of the terracing. Before each home game, a member of staff would proudly raise the club flag with 'City FC' on and then lower it after the match had ended.

Surprisingly, City only once went an entire league season at Maine Road without defeat – during the 1965/66 campaign – when the club went up as

Marsh

CONTROVERSY, TERRIFIC INDI-vidual skill and frustration – the mercurial Rodney Marsh had the City fans eating out of his hand and tearing out their hair in equal measures for much of his time at the club. Signed from QPR to boost City's 1972 title run-in, he was blamed by many for City's disappointing finish to the season. Despite playing during a period packed with personalities and stars, his sublime skills and invention still shone brightly and he went on to play 142 times for the Blues, scoring on 46 occasions.

A fall-out with boss Tony Book led to him being dropped from the first team and he was transfer-listed after being accused of not giving 100 per cent – something he vehemently denied. He almost moved to Anderlecht during November 1975 after the two clubs agreed a fee but he decided the language could be a problem and stayed at Maine Road, training with the youth team until the dispute was

LEFT Rodney Marsh, 1973

settled. In 1976, he finally ended his City career by moving to Tampa Bay Rowdies as one of the first English players to join the blossoming NASL. He continued to sparkle throughout his career and, during a brief time period with Fulham in the mid-Seventies (along with George Best), he produced showmanship of the highest calibre. Today, controversial as ever, Rodney splits his time between London and Florida, and for those who remember his days in a sky-blue jersey, they probably wouldn't want him to be any other way.

RIGHT Rodney Marsh in training

McDowall

LES MCDOWALL SPENT A FAIR proportion of his life employed by Manchester City – 24 years in fact – though his playing days were truncated by the Second World War. Born in Gunga Pur, India, it was the 1930s' Depression that first brought McDowall into the spotlight. An aircraft draughtsman, he was laid off due to lack of work and was playing a match with other unemployed men when a scout from Sunderland spotted him. He signed for Sunderland and played 13 games for the Roker Park outfit until City came in with a bid of around £7,500 in 1938.

Within a year McDowall was made skipper of the Blues up until war broke out, ironically putting his football career on hold while he returned to his former trade. Times changed and following the war he handed over the captaincy to Sam Barkas and not long after he was briefly appointed manager

of Wrexham. A little over a year later and City returned for their former captain – this time with the offer of being manager with an immediate challenge of hauling the club out of Division Two. It would be a historic appointment in many ways as his tenure

RIGHT Les McDowall watches on as Denis Law signs for City

was never short of excitement and drama. In charge for some 13 years, he was also, behind Wilf Wild, just one year short of managing the club for a record length of time.

Never afraid to adopt innovative ideas, he was in charge when the famous 'Revie Plan' was instigated and he began his reign with instant promotion. He also tried the little publicised 'Marsden Plan', which involved Keith Marsden acting as a sweeper. City lost 6-1 to Preston and 9-2 to West Brom and the plan was indefinitely shelved! More positively, the club went on to successive FA Cup finals in 1955 and 1956 under McDowall; the latter of which was victorious. Players such as Denis Law were signed during his reign and in 1960 Law's £55,000 transfer fee was a British record. City eventually were relegated under McDowall and in 1963, after presiding over an incredible 546 league games, he left for Oldham Athletic, where he stayed for two years. He died in 1991, aged 78.

Mercer

IF SUCCESS IS GAUGED BY HOW many trophies your team wins, Joe Mercer is the greatest City manager of them all. Regarded by many as one of the greatest wing-halves of his day, Joe was an Everton player from 1932 until 1947, collecting a League Championship medal in 1939. The war stole many years from him and when the League resumed, things had changed at Goodison Park and he moved to Highbury.

With Arsenal he went on to even greater glory, including two more League Championships plus another winner's medal for clinching the FA Cup. A broken leg forced retirement and robbed him of yet more playing years. His first move into management was with Sheffield United and he impressed sufficiently to be later installed as Aston Villa boss. He took them to promotion from Division Two, won the League Cup and led them to two FA Cup semi-finals. The pressures and stress of management took their toll on him and he suffered a minor stroke, threatening his future in the game he had already given so much to. Fortunately, fate had cleared a path that would take him on to yet greater heights, and after the doctors gave him a clean bill of health, the Villa board duly sacked him! He decided to retire and many thought they had seen

BELOW Joe Mercer, 1957

RIGHT Joe Mercer
holds aloft the League
Championship trophy,
1968

the last of 'Genial Joe'. But Mercer's love of the game pulled him back and in 1965, when Manchester City offered him the opportunity of waking a sleeping giant, he grabbed the chance with both hands.

His first decision as Blues' boss was also arguably his best, bringing in upcoming coach Malcolm Allison as his assistant and though the pair were as alike as chalk and cheese, they would prove the perfect managerial team – as good as any in the history of English football. Within a year, Mercer's new-look City side had won the Division Two title, and two years later the Blues were crowned champions of England for only the second time in the club's history, winning the First Division with the style and panache the supporters demanded.

The trophies just kept on coming. The FA Cup in 1969, the League Cup in 1970 and later that same season, the first and only European trophy City have won – the Cup Winners' Cup – was brought back to Manchester by Mercer and his talented troops. Five trophies in five years – an incredible return. Malcolm Allison was involved in some bitter arguments with the City board

BELOW Malcolm
Allison and Joe Mercer

and in 1970 he was very nearly sacked, but, with Joe Mercer's backing, Allison remained at the club. City almost added another league title in season 1971/72, but Allison's idea of bringing in Rodney Marsh backfired and City lost pole position to end fourth in one of the tightest top-flight finishes ever. After seven years as number two, Allison seemingly manipulated events that led to Mercer leaving his position and eventually joining Coventry City in 1972. Allison believed he deserved a chance to call the shots himself and though nobody would have denied him the chance, many were upset by the events leading to Mercer's departure.

A general manager at Coventry, he became England boss on a temporary basis in 1974 in order to, as he put it himself, 'try and restore some laughter' following the national side's omission from the World Cup qualifiers. He was deservedly awarded the OBE in 1976 for services to football and he remained as a director at Highfield Road until his resignation in 1981. He retired to his beloved Merseyside and died in August 1990. A legendary and much-loved figure to all Manchester City fans, the club recently named an access road to the City of Manchester Stadium 'Joe Mercer Way'.

Meredith

BORN IN CHIRK, NORTH WALES, Billy Meredith used to cycle from his tiny mining village to Hyde Road to play for City and then cycle home afterwards. He is also, without doubt, one of the greatest players ever to represent Manchester City. Meredith was something of a controversial character, but is ranked by many alongside the great

Sir Stanley Matthews in stature and an icon for all football fans and the media in his day. Bandy-legged and invariably chewing a toothpick, Meredith was a fantastic player and the scourge of many an Edwardian defender. The immensely talented right-winger could pinpoint a cross for a forward or cut inside and lash the ball home himself if the mood took him and despite hugging the touchline for much of the game, with 151 goals for the club, he is among the all-time top scorers for City. He was involved in a bribe and illegal payment scandal that rocked the club to its foundations and he eventually joined Manchester United, helping them to great success before finally returning to City in 1921. He also won 22 Welsh caps as a City player and holds the record for being the oldest footballer to turn out for the Blues. He was aged just 120 days short of his 50th birthday in his last game for the club – a 2-0 defeat to Newcastle United in an FA Cup semi-final and it was Meredith who effectively was the founder member of the Players Football Association (PFA) just over 100 years ago.

RIGHT Billy Meredith, 1920

Morrison

ANDY MORRISON ARRIVED AT Maine Road in 1998 like a raging bull and manager Joe Royle would later claim it was Morrison who dragged City 'kicking and screaming' to promotion from Division Two in 1999. A natural leader, Morrison was the streak of steel missing from City's armour at a time when the younger players desperately needed guidance and somebody to encourage them while being prepared to tear a strip off them if they needed it, too. Costing a mere £80,000 from Huddersfield Town, Royle initially brought Morrison to City on loan, but the impact he had was so great as was the demand from the fans to secure his services on a permanent basis, that he'd signed the strapping Scot before the

LEFT Andy Morrison holds off Dele Adebola of Birmingham City, 2001

RIGHT Andy Morrison
lifts the play-off trophy,
1999

loan period had barely started. He was soon made captain and started with three goals in his first four games, including a spectacular volley in a 3-0 win at Oldham.

Morrison was soon a huge crowd favourite as fans tapped in to the passion he showed playing for their club. 'Mozzer' as everyone knew him, was rarely beaten in the air, was an excellent passer of the ball and was fearsome in the tackle. His inspirational qualities as captain guided City into the Division Two play-offs and after a tense semifinal victory over Wigan Athletic, he led the Blues out against Gillingham, for what was to be one of the most dramatic matches Wembley had ever seen. Injury blighted his remaining years at Maine Road and in 2002 he and City parted company amicably but despite making less than

50 starts for the club, he is still regarded as one of the most inspirational captains of all time.

Nil

CITY CREATED A PIECE OF unwanted history when they went eight consecutive Premiership home games without scoring in season 2006/07. It meant that City had only managed to score in seven of their home games all season, 12 ending without a goal for the home side and earning the Blues the nickname 'Manchester City nil' within media circles. In a generally poor season for scoring all round, it was the lowest goals tally the club has ever had with the top scorer, Joey Barton, ending with a paltry six. On the flipside, the 14 clean sheets City kept during 2006/07 is the club's highest tally in the Premiership.

LEFT Joey Barton looks dejected after he missed a penalty during a Premiership match against Aston Villa, 2007

Oakes

ALAN OAKES GAVE SOLID, RELIable service to Manchester City as a player for more than 18 years. With 669 first-team appearances, he is the record appearance holder and is unlikely ever to be surpassed. Surprisingly overlooked at international level for England, due almost entirely to the fact that he played a similar role to the legendary Bobby Moore, Oakes was every bit as important to City as Moore was to West Ham. His cousin was another unsung hero from the same era, Glyn Pardoe. Best known for his surging runs from deep and penetrative passes, Oakes was happy to let others take the limelight yet was vital to the glorious all-conquering Mercer side of the late 1960s and the management showed their faith in Oakes by naming him captain for the 1968-69 season in Tony Book's absence.

He almost won international recognition when he was one of several City players named in the original squad of 40 for the 1970 World Cup, but missed out on a trip to Mexico when the final squad was named. Consistent up until the end of his days at Maine Road, he was named Player of the Year in 1975, just a year before he left City for Chester, where he eventually became player-manager of the club and added another 211 appearances to his career total.

Oasis

BURNAGE-BORN BRO-thers Noel and Liam Gallagher, the driving forces behind rock band Oasis, are perhaps City's most famous supporters. During the mid-1990s, the band and the club enjoyed a healthy association, lending branding and suchlike to one another in a mutually beneficial relationship. For a while, City ran out to 'Roll with It' and it was rare for an Oasis record not to be playing during the half-time break at Maine Road. The Gallaghers walked out on the pitch on several occasions and Noel even had a specially-made 'MCFC' guitar.

In 1995 the City support turned their classic 'Wonderwall' into a swooning tribute to Georgi Kinkladze and Alan Ball, though Noel commented that he wasn't too happy about the Alan Ball verse! The culmination of mutual admiration between band and club reached epidemic proportions when Oasis played several sold-out gigs at Maine Road in 1996 and were even once touted as potential owners. Though the band moved down to London, the brothers were at the 1999 play-off final and regularly attend matches played in the south. In 2006 they played more concerts in Manchester, this time at City's new stadium.

BELOW Liam (R) and Noel Gallagher, 2005

Pardoe

THOUGH GLYN PARDOE PLAYED in almost every position for City during his long career at the club, it was left-back that was his preferred role. The cousin of another City great, Alan Oakes, Pardoe was also part of the all-conquering City side of the late 1960s and early 1970s that swept all before them. Like Oakes, Pardoe, born in Winsford, joined from Mid-Cheshire Boys. Arguably his finest moment came when he scored the winner in the 1970 League Cup final, one of only 22 goals during his time at Maine Road.

He was desperately unlucky when he broke his leg in the Manchester derby later that same year, following a horrific challenge by George Best, and never managed to fully reclaim his left-back berth owing to the form of youngster Willie Donachie. The holder of two unique records, being the youngest player to ever play for the Blues aged just 15, Pardoe was also the Blues' first ever substitute (unused) for the opening game of the 1965-66 season. He later became a hugely successful youth-team coach at Maine Road following his retirement in 1976, helping guide the young Blues to win the 1986 FA Youth Cup.

Paul

MANCHESTER CITY'S VERY OWN Captain Fantastic, Roy Paul was an inspirational figure to colleagues and fans alike, captaining the Blues to the 1955 FA Cup final, where they lost to Newcastle United. The hard as nails Paul then vowed to return to win the Cup the following year and, true to his word, the former coal miner drove the Blues on to the 1956 FA Cup final after threatening to clip around the ear anybody who didn't pull their weight. It

PAUL

LEFT Roy Paul pictured with his son after winning the FA Cup, 1956

BELOW LEFT Roy Paul holds the FA Cup aloft in victory as his teammates carry him in a victory lap, 1956

worked, and this time City were victorious over Birmingham City. Paul, who handed his own brand of justice out on the pitch – fairly – had arrived

from Swansea Town in 1950 and was versatile in that he could play anywhere across the back line. A true 'Roy of the Rovers'-type player, Paul is one of the greatest captains the club has ever had and he was the second Welshman to skipper the Blues to FA Cup glory – the first being Billy Meredith. Paul left for Worcester City in June 1957 after clocking up nearly 300 matches for City. He died in the spring of 2002.

Penalties

CITY HAVE HAD, SHALL WE SAY, their moments from the penalty spot, both good and bad. In 1912, City

managed to miss three penalties in one game! Irvine Thornley and Eli Fletcher (twice) were the guilty parties and the game with Newcastle ended 1-1. It was Newcastle who were again the opposition on another unfortunate day from the spot, this time for Billy Austin, when in 1926, the Blues, who needed a point to avoid relegation after five successive wins, missed from the spot and lost 3-2 and were subsequently relegated! Ken Barnes scored a hat-trick of penalties against Everton in December 1957 in a 6-2 victory and scored another in the return fixture at Goodison Park. Mention penalties to any City fan, however, and chances are talk will quickly get around to Franny Lee – the club's most successful penalty-taker ever with 46 spot-kicks successfully dispatched in his time at Maine Road. Lee won many of the penalties himself and was deadly from the spot. Dennis Tueart scored an impressive 24 times from the spot, including several double strikes. Kevin

RIGHT Dennis Tueart, 1981

Bond once scored penalties in the 44th and 45th minutes of a home game against Huddersfield Town. In 2006, Arsenal were awarded a penalty against City and Thierry Henry ran up, tapped the ball forward for Robert Pires to put past David James – at least, that's what was meant to happen! The Gunners stars made a hash of the chance and Danny Mills cleared the ball down field. Though the City players were furious at such a seemingly disrespectful act, the Blues had actually done something similar more than 40 years before. In March 1960 when Denis Law made his home debut against West Ham and with City trailing 1-0, Law was fouled in the box and the Blues were awarded a penalty. Ken Barnes placed the ball on the spot, ran up and tapped it forward for Billy McAdams to run from behind and tuck the ball away. The referee gave the goal but amidst furious protests from the Hammers, he consulted a linesman and

LEFT Francis Lee, 1971

ordered the kick to be retaken. Barnes stepped up again and missed! Fortunately, City went on to win 3-1.

Player of the Year

The list of Player of the Year awards that began following the completion of the 1966-67 season, as voted by the club's supporters, is as follows:

1966-67: Tony Book
1967-68: Colin Bell
1968-69: Glyn Pardoe
1969-70: Francis Lee
1970-71: Mike Doyle
1971-72: Mike Summerbee
1972-73: Mike Summerbee
1973-74: Mike Doyle
1974-75: Alan Oakes
1975-76: Joe Corrigan
1976-77: Dave Watson
1977-78: Joe Corrigan
1978-79: Asa Hartford
1979-80: Joe Corrigan
1980-81: Paul Power
1981-82: Tommy Caton
1982-83: Kevin Bond
1983-84: Mick McCarthy
1984-85: Paul Power
1985-86: Kenny Clements

1986-87: Neil McNab
1987-88: Steve Redmond
1988-89: Neil McNab
1989-90: Colin Hendry
1990-91: Niall Quinn
1991-92: Tony Coton
1992-93: Garry Flitcroft
1993-94: Tony Coton
1994-95: Uwe Rosler
1995-96: Gio Kinkladze
1996-97: Gio Kinkladze
1997-98: Michael Brown
1998-99: Gerard Wiekens
1999-00: Shaun Goater
2000-01: Danny Tiatto
2001-02: Ali Benarbia
2002-03: Sylvain Distin
2003-04: Shaun Wright-Phillips
2004-05: Richard Dunne
2005-06: Richard Dunne
2006-07: Richard Dunne

Power

PAUL POWER WAS POSSIBLY one of the hardest-working City players ever to pull on a blue shirt and he captained the club for many years, earning respect throughout the game for being one of the most dedicated professionals in football. The left-sided defender or midfielder might not have been a prolific scorer for the Blues, but he is best remembered by City fans for two incredible goals he scored during his time with the club. His wonderful solo goal against AC Milan in 1978 in the San Siro stadium gave the Blues a vital edge in a difficult UEFA Cup tie and his superb curling free-kick against Ipswich in the 1981 FA Cup semi-final sent City to Wembley to face Tottenham in the Centenary Cup final. His services were rewarded by City supporters who twice voted him Player of the Year and he captained the Blues in three Wembley Cup finals – twice against Spurs in the FA Cup and once against Chelsea in the Full Members' Cup. An intelligent and thoughtful man, he qualified in law after completing his studies in 1975. He was sold to Everton by manager Billy McNeill in June 1986 and waited only 12 months before picking up his first League Championship medal with the Toffees. He has been one of the senior Academy coaches at Platt Lane for several years, now, passing on valuable experience to the next generation of City stars.

BELOW Paul Power

Quinn

Q

RIGHT Niall Quinn playing against Leicester City, 1994

NIALL QUINN JOINED FROM Arsenal for a bargain £800,000 in 1989 and went on to become one the most popular players to ever wear the No 9 shirt for the club. His skilful and intelligent link-up play belied his 6ft 4in, with his deft flicks, chips and cushioned headers backed by excellent technique. He was often a valuable extra defender at set pieces and corners, and one abiding memory City fans have of 'Quinny' was the time he took over in goal during a home match with Derby County after keeper Tony Coton had brought down Dean Saunders and was shown a red card. With no goalie on the bench, Quinn, a former Gaelic football player, put on the green jersey to face the penalty kick. With the whole of Maine Road willing him on, he guessed right and saved the penalty from Saunders! His two goals in the final match of the same season relegated Sunderland, the club he would eventually join in 1996 and become chairman of a decade later. Quinn also commendably donated the entire proceeds of his testimonial – believed to have been around £1 million – to charity. An excellent servant for Manchester City and Ireland.

Reid

WHEN HOWARD KENDALL BECAME City manager in November 1989, he had only one man in mind to lead his side out of the relegation battle – Peter Reid. Installed as player/coach, Reid had the natural leadership qualities that City desperately needed, and though he may have had his best years elsewhere, the gutsy little midfielder never gave less than his all for City, and the fans loved him for it.

Reid held together a young midfield and influenced a side with a reputation for having something of a soft centre, into a tight, difficult-to-beat dogs of war outfit and when Howard Kendall quit the Blues after just a year in charge, Reid seemed the natural successor and by popular demand, he became the club's first player/manager, guiding them to successive fifth-placed finishes in the League.

Things turned sour for Reid when, it is alleged, the board asked him to dispense with the services of his coach Sam Ellis, the man the fans blamed for the long-ball game City were by that time playing. Reid refused to be forced into a corner and was sacked as a result, loyally standing by Ellis. The football being played at the time was neither attractive nor entertaining and a move for Reid was probably best for everybody.

ABOVE Peter Reid, 1991

Richards

BORN IN BIRMINGHAM, BUT RAISED
in Leeds, Micah Richards burst into the
City first team having played just a
handful of reserve games for City. An
outstanding Academy player, he made
his Premiership debut against Arsenal
in October 2005, aged 17. He first came
to the attention of the nation when he
scored a last minute equaliser for City
in an FA Cup tie at Aston Villa and
promptly swore during the after-match
interview! A powerfully-built lad, he is
comfortable in almost any position
and his whirlwind rise to the top continued when he was awarded a full cap
against Holland during the 2006/07
season, becoming the youngest
defender to ever play for England.
Richards was an integral part of City's
defence during his first full season,
winning plaudits throughout the game
for his strength and athleticism. He
was also the youngest nominee for the
PFA Young Player of the Year award
2007 and, at the time of writing, he is
perhaps the most coveted young player
in the country.

RIGHT Micah Richards
(L) vies with Chelsea's
Arjen Robben, 2007

FAR RIGHT
Uwe Rosler in action

Rosler

GERMAN STRIKER UWE ROSLER – 'Der Bomber' – was, ironically, a typically English centre-forward whose bustling energetic style made his £500,000 fee from FC Nurnberg look like peanuts after finishing top scorer in three of four full seasons with the Blues. The fans immediately identified with Rosler's passion and he became a huge crowd idol on the Kippax with his strike partnership with Paul Walsh particularly profitable, especially when serviced by a constant stream of superb crosses from wingers Peter Beagrie and Nicky Summerbee. Rosler was lethal in the air and went on to win caps for Germany after winning several from East Germany prior to unification. He returned home to play for Kaiserslautern after City were relegated to Division Two in 1998, but failed to repeat the heroics he showed while at Maine Road with either them, West Brom or Southampton. Rosler made a successful recovery from chest cancer while playing for Lillestrøm in Norway and would later manage the same club.

Royle

SIGNED FROM EVERTON ON Christmas Eve 1974 for £200,000, Joe Royle became an integral part of Tony

Book's successful mid-1970s side, leading the line bravely and often being the foil for Dennis Tueart or Brian Kidd. Never a prolific scorer, he finished the season with just 1 goal from 16 games – it was to be his one failing during his

RIGHT Joe Royle (R) celebrates Peter Barnes' (L) goal with him and team-mate Dennis Tueart

time with the Blues as a player, where he averaged just one every four games.

After leaving City he played for Bristol City and Norwich before moving into management with Oldham Athletic where he transformed a music hall joke of a club into one of the most respected sides in the country. He later managed Everton, guiding them to an FA Cup final before taking charge of City in 1998. Though he seemed to have arrived with time to save the club, City were still relegated and Royle and his assistant Willie Donachie began to trim the unusually large squad and build a new one from scratch. Gio Kinkladze was sold to Ajax for £5.5 million while the likes of Andy Morrison, Ian Bishop and Shaun Goater were all recruited for less than half a million pounds in total.

Under Royle, City would then secure back-to-back promotions after beating Gillingham in the Division Two play-off final and finishing runners-up to Charlton

LEFT Joe Royle, 1991

Athletic the following season. Royle was a hero and could do little wrong in the supporters' eyes. With the likes of George Weah and Paulo Wanchope signed during the summer of 2000, the Blues faced up to life in the Premiership with confidence, but 10 months later City had been relegated. Surprisingly, Royle was sacked in May 2001 and replaced by Kevin Keegan. It was a sad end for Big Joe, who it seemed, at one point, could do no wrong.

Summerbee

MIKE SUMMERBEE IS ONE of (if not the) greatest wingers that has played for Manchester City. 'Buzzer' – as one and all knew him – was a vital member of the Joe Mercer side of the late 1960s and his contribution to the Blues' halcyon days was immense. Adored by the crowd, especially the Kippax, Summerbee played the game with good humour and was happy to entertain the Maine Road faithful with or without the ball, though his professionalism or will to win were never compromised in the least. With Colin Bell and Franny Lee, he was part of the so-called "Holy Trinity" that inspired City to success after success. Along with Lee, he became one of the first attackers to defend from

the front, often seeking out his marker early on and then launching into a crunching tackle. With Summerbee there was never a dull moment. Though far from a prolific scorer, he made many goals for others and he was also the first City star to be voted Player of the Year for two successive years in 1972 and 1973. Something of a fashion icon, he owned a successful shirt-tailoring company for many years and once co-owned a fashion boutique with George Best, but it will always be on the pitch that the former England star will be most fondly remembered.

Swift

SIGNED FROM NON-LEAGUE Fleetwood Town after he'd written to Maine Road to ask for a trial, Frank Swift's career spanned 17 years and Manchester City were the only club he ever played for. Swift was only the second goalkeeper to captain England and was the innovator of many unorthodox ideas including the long throw-out instead of a hoof up the pitch – Swift could comfortably grip the ball in one hand. He enjoyed a run of four seasons when he was an ever-present in

the team and would be likely to hold the record appearances for City, but for the unavoidable break of seven seasons, due to the Second World War. Swift was a gentle giant and was adored by the supporters, especially the youngsters, who idolised him. He retired in 1949 and was replaced by Bert Trautmann, eventually moving into journalism. It was after covering Manchester United's game in Yugoslavia that one of City's greatest ever players lost his life in the 1958 Munich air disaster – a tragic end to a hugely talented and popular man.

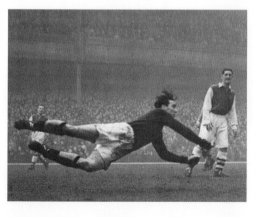

Toseland

ERNIE TOSELAND JOINED CITY from Coventry in 1929 after scoring 11 goals in 22 appearances for the Sky Blues. The flying winger then went on to become a vital part of the Blues' championship and FA Cup-winning side of the 1930s. Unlucky to never win full England honours, Toseland was at his peak at a time of many other great wingers and it is likely that for this reason alone he never had the chance to shine on an international level. He rarely missed a game during his time at Maine Road and his goal tally regularly reached double figures for the Blues. He played in successive FA Cup finals for City in 1933 and 1934, scoring four times and playing in all rounds during the successful return to Wembley against Portsmouth. Along with Eric Brook, Alec Herd and Fred Tilson, Toseland forged one of the most feared attacks in the game and with 409 appearances for City over a 10-year period; he is also one of the club's greatest servants.

LEFT Ernie Toseland, 1931

Trautmann

BERT TRAUTMANN OVERCAME A whole host of incredible obstacles to become one of the most popular players ever to play for the Blues. A German paratrooper during the Second World War, Trautmann was captured in Normandy and then made a prisoner-of-war. While at the POW camp in Ashton-in-Makerfield, he tried his hand at goalkeeping. His training as a para-trooper had served him well, as he would later claim that it helped him dive around fearlessly without getting hurt and when he was released after the war, he decided to stay in England, eventually finding work on a farm. He played for St Helens FC and shortly after married the club secretary's daughter. Word had spread of the fantastic German goal-keeper, though much of the interest was curiosity initially, with the war still fresh in everyone's minds. With Frank Swift now retired, the Blues moved quickly to sign

RIGHT Bert Trautmann makes a fine save against West Ham United, 1959

FAR RIGHT Making a save during a game against Arsenal, 1955

Trautmann after a trial though some City fans were at first resentful of the German's presence in the team, especially as he was the replacement for the revered Swift. However, he soon won over the doubters, and they were quick to recognise him as a man with the heart of a lion. Incredibly, while helping City to a 1956 FA Cup final victory over Birmingham, he dived bravely at a Birmingham striker's legs and hurt himself badly. He had, in fact, broken his neck, yet he continued playing, despite the obvious agony he was in. Doctors later told him he was within an inch of death, yet he still climbed the steps to collect his winner's medal though obviously in a lot of discomfort. Such heroism will never be forgotten and some years later at his testimonial, a huge crowd, believed to be around 60,000 in number, turned up to pay their respects. A true Manchester City legend.

Tueart

SIGNED BY CITY BOSS RON Saunders in March 1974, Dennis Tueart became the club's record signing when

he arrived from Sunderland for £275,000. The fiery winger soon settled into the side and it wasn't long before he became a big crowd favourite, with his aggressive, never-say-die attitude complementing perfectly his dazzling

skills and eye for a spectacular goal. If he was popular going into the 1976 League Cup final against Newcastle, he came out of it all but immortal after his spectacular overhead kick won the game 2-1. A penalty expert and scorer of several hat-tricks – three in one season, Tueart was a particular favourite among the club's younger fans.

Never one to allow the grass to grow under his feet, he left for New York Cosmos in 1978 and again became a hero to the vast crowds that crammed into the Meadowlands Stadium in the Big Apple. A Tueart goal would be welcomed by an electronic board message of 'Sweet Feet' or 'Do it, Tueart!'

Playing alongside some of the world's best players and living a life of luxury, complete with Cadillac, Dennis enjoyed almost two years in the USA before he rejoined City for £150,000 and came back to his adopted home of Manchester for good. Over the next three seasons he scored 22 goals in 66 starts, this despite a serious Achilles injury. He left

LEFT Dennis Tueart at Heathrow, during his time with the Cosmos

the Blues in 1983 as part of a wage-trimming exercise, bound for Stoke, as the club faced up to life in the Second Division. He returned to the club for a third time in 1997 as a City director.

UEFA Cup

CITY'S FIRST FORAY IN THE UEFA Cup, formerly known as the Fairs Cup, was in 1972-73 when they took on Spaniards Valencia at Maine Road. The game ended 2-2 with goals from Ian Mellor and Rodney Marsh. The second leg ended the Blues' interest in the tournament with a 2-1 defeat and it wasn't until four years later, in 1976-77, that the Blues again bowed out in the first round, this time to all-conquering Italian side Juventus. A solitary goal, courtesy of a Brian Kidd header, was never going to be enough against a cynical and superbly organized side and there were no surprises when the Blues lost 2-0 in Turin to crash out of the competition. At least City could console

RIGHT
Paulo Wanchope clashes with Lumir Sedlacek and Sebastian Mila of Groclin during the UEFA Cup second round, first leg match, 2003

themselves with the fact Juventus went on to win the competition. The first-round curse continued the following year when Polish side Widzew Lodz held City 2-2 in the first leg and 0-0 in the second, meaning that City were out on the away-goals rule.

By far the most enjoyable UEFA Cup campaign came during season 1978-79. City saw off Dutch side FC Twente and then confidently dispatched Belgian side Standard Liège to set up a tantalizing clash with AC Milan, and the Blues sensationally went 2-0 ahead at the San Siro through Paul Power and Brian Kidd. Milan fought back for 2-2, but the result was heralded as one of the best by an English side in Europe and, inspired for the return game, City won 3-0. German outfit Borussia Mönchengladbach were next up in the quarter-final, but after they earned a 1-1 draw at Maine Road, the tie seemed all but over, and so it proved as the Germans won the second leg won 3-1 and, just as Juventus had done before, City's victors would go on

to win the UEFA Cup. In 2003, the Blues qualified for the UEFA Cup via the Fair Play League and saw off Total Network Solutions and Lokeren before going out to Polish side Groclin Dyskobolia.

ABOVE Joey Barton (L) in action against Radek Mynar from Groclin during the second round, second leg UEFA Cup match, 2003

Varadi

JOURNEYMAN STRIKER IMRE VARADI became a Manchester City cult hero during his two-year stay with the club. Varadi, who had a decent track record at his previous clubs, was signed to inject some much-needed imagination into a sterile attack. With only four goals in nine games, boss Jimmy Frizzell had sold ineffective strikers Gordon Davies and Trevor Christie and agreed a straight swap with West Brom, with the disappointing Robert Hopkins moving to The Hawthorns and Varadi coming to City. He made his debut in a 2-1 defeat at Chelsea, scoring City's only goal and immediately showing the predatory instincts the Blues had been sadly lacking. With youth team product Paul Moulden partnering Varadi, the pair inspired a four-match unbeaten run for the Blues. City still couldn't avoid the inevitable relegation back to Division Two.

Paul Stewart was signed from Blackpool by new manager Mel Machin and emerging youth-team product David White was by now also knocking on the first-team door, and along with another new arrival, Tony Adcock, from having no strikers of any worth, City suddenly had several decent forwards vying for a first-team spot. With a return of nine goals from a dozen starts, Varadi started the 1987/88 campaign as first-choice striker on merit and by this time was proving a huge hit on the terraces. Some say the chanting of his name led to the first inflatable banana appearing at Maine Road for one home game and thus followed a chant of 'Imre Banana'! Typically, Varadi was sidelined for the 10-1 mauling of

ABOVE Imre Varadi

Huddersfield Town and found it difficult to break back into the side there-
after. When he did, it took him three
months to score again and in 1989 he
returned to one of his former clubs,
Sheffield Wednesday.

Watson

RIGHT Dave Watson, 1973

WHEN YOU HEAR PEOPLE at matches say 'they don't make them like that, any more', chances are they are thinking of footballers like Dave Watson. A man-mountain of a centre-back, Watson was signed from Sunderland in 1975 where he'd earned the unusual distinction of being a full England international without ever playing in the top division. The towering defender took no time to settle at Maine Road and he formed a tremendous partnership with skipper Mike Doyle, particularly during the 1976-77 season, which saw City come within a point of winning the First Division title. Watson was 28 years old when he signed and, fortunately for City, the following four seasons would prove to be arguably the best of his career. Commanding in the air and crunching in the tackle, Watson presented a formidable challenge for any forwards in England and he would win a further 30 England caps while at Maine Road before eventually being sold to German club Werder Bremen during Malcolm Allison's second spell at City.

Weaver

NICK WEAVER WROTE HIS NAME into the history books of Manchester City with a meteoric rise that took him to the verge of full England honours during his first few years at the club. Weaver played a vital role in City's successive promotions to the Premier League and became a household name as he saved the penalty that won the 1999 play-off final against Gillingham. His celebratory run saw him skirt the challenges of several team-mates before being felled unceremoniously by Andy Morrison. A regular in the England Under-21 team, Weaver was at his best as the Blues raced to promotion from Division One in 1999-2000 but his form dipped the following campaign and he was forced to share first-team duties with Carlo Nash. Weaver then suffered a succession of career-threatening knee injuries that saw him miss the best part of three years before revolutionary transplant surgery in America saw him come back

in 2005/06 and enjoy a successful loan spell at Sheffield Wednesday. His dramatic turnaround in fortunes came full circle when he seemed to have established himself as first choice keeper again during the 2006/07 season, with his form as good as at any time during his career. It was his tenth year with the Blues and throughout that time, his popularity never wavered, though towards the end of that campaign, Andreas Isaksson seemed to have finished in pole position.

BELOW Nicky Weaver celebrates his team's 2-1 victory over Leeds, 2000

RIGHT David White
jumps over Tony Adams
of Arsenal for the ball
during a Division One
match, 1991

White

DAVID WHITE HAD TO OVER-
come his nerves to establish himself as
one of the Blues' best modern-day
forwards. Blessed with electric pace, the
young right-winger was part of the FA
Youth Cup-winning team of 1985-86
and he also burst into the seniors
the following season, playing on 24
occasions but scoring only once.

Being pitched in at the deep end into
a struggling side heading for relegation
did little for his confidence and he was
taken out of the side for a time to
rebuild his self-belief. Mel Machin
decided to make White a regular as the
club battled to return to Division One,
and White played 40 times, netting 13 in
his first full campaign with his pace and
finishing a constant threat to opposing
teams. His blistering speed was one of
the main reasons City destroyed
Huddersfield in 1987 and White
famously scored goal number 10 in the
10-1 win, completing his own hat-trick
in the process.

An explosive player, he could also
frustrate on occasions, with his finishing varying from the sublime to awful.

He alternated between wide-right and more central roles and became an important part of the Blues' side in the late 1980s and early 1990s forging a deadly partnership with Niall Quinn and profiting from the big Irishman's flicks in much the same way as Kevin Phillips would later do at Sunderland. As a testament to his consistency in front of goal, White hit 15, 18 and 16 goals with Quinn alongside and City raced to successive top five finishes in 1991 and 1992. He won his one and only England cap in 1992, but failed to impress in a defeat against Spain.

White joined Leeds in December 1993 as part of a £2 million exchange that brought David Rocastle to Maine Road. He never repeated his heroics for the Elland Road side and later moved to Sheffield United. His best days were undoubtedly in a sky-blue shirt and with 96 goals and more than 300 appearances for the Blues, he fits snugly into the category of great modern-day City players.

Woosnam

THERE HAVE BEEN FEW SPORT-ing all-rounders produced in Britain that could match the man they called 'Gentleman' Max Woosnam. Woosnam joined City from the famous amateur side Corinthians in November 1919, and this was his first professional club. A Cambridge Blue at golf, tennis and foot-ball, he also won a Wimbledon doubles title and an Olympic gold medal for tennis. Popular, and the perfect gentle-man, hence the nickname, he even on occasion carried a handkerchief around the pitch to befit his image. Born in Liverpool, the handsome, strapping defender immediately gave City's back-line a classy look and he never gave less than one hundred per cent – the drive that had made him such a winner in so many different disciplines. Well-groomed, immaculately dressed and respected by all, Woosnam was a huge success with the City fans and went on to captain both City and England. He was also a pioneer of amateurs being allowed to play with professionals, increasing his popularity even more within the game, especially when he took a stand against the Amateur Football Association over the matter. He broke his leg on a fence that surrounded Hyde Road in 1922 and in October 1925 he left for Northwich Victoria, having made a lasting impression on the Blues.

X-tra Time

EXTRA TIME HAS BEEN BOTH KIND and cruel to City over the years. One of the first memorable instances was when the Blues locked horns with Portuguese side Academica Coimbra in the quarter-final of the European Cup Winners' Cup. With no goal scored in either leg, extra time was almost up at Maine Road when Tony Towers struck with just seconds remaining to send City through to the semi-finals. The 1981 FA Cup final went into extra time, too, but despite the Blues having the better chances, the score remained 1-1 and went to a replay. Extra-time periods in League Cup matches have seen City fail to score against Stoke, Blackpool and Doncaster, winning at Stoke on penalties but losing miserably to Blackpool and Doncaster by the same sudden-death method. City's dramatic comeback in the 1999 play-off final against Gillingham ensured an extra half-hour of play, often forgotten amid all the chaos, but it passed without either side really threatening and the Blues instead triumphed on penalties.

BELOW Manchester City players celebrate promotion and victory after a penalty shoot-out, 1999

Young

V

RIGHT Neil Young beats Peter Shilton with a winning goal, 1969

GIFTED, ELEGANT AND A wonderful footballer – are descriptions attributed to Neil Young during a glorious career with Manchester City. Young played a number of key roles in the City forward line before Joe Mercer gave him the No 10 shirt for keeps and then contentedly sat back as the Manchester-born striker began to fulfil his considerable potential. Young, better known to the City fans as 'Nellie' possessed a lethal yet cultured left foot and was a key member of the City side that swept all in its path in the late Sixties and early Seventies. In fact, it could be argued that Young had a more substantial role than anyone else during that era, having scored crucial goals at times when important matches were finely balanced.

He was also the top scorer when the Blues last lifted the Division One Championship trophy with 19, and bagged a couple in the final and deciding game at Newcastle United. It was Young's left-foot cracker that won the 1969 FA Cup final against Leicester City and he was, without doubt, a major influence in City's European Cup Winners' Cup triumph a year later after scoring and then winning a penalty in the 2-1 win over Gornik Zabrze. Young was mystifyingly overlooked at international level, but his place with the heroes of yesteryear is guaranteed among all Blues followers, many of whom still refer to him in revered tones. Young signed for Preston in January 1972 for £48,000 after 13 years at Maine Road.

Youth Cup

THE CLUB'S YOUTH TEAM HAS WON the coveted FA Youth Cup on only one occasion, but have been one of the forces of youth football for many years. In 1986 both City and Manchester United made it to the two-legged final. The first leg, watched by just 7,602, ended 1-1 at Old Trafford with Paul Lake scoring for City. The second leg at Maine Road was watched by 18,164 partisan City supporters, who roared the young Blues on to a 2-0 win, with goals from Moulden and Boyd. City had previously reached the final in 1978-79 and 1979-80 but on both occasions were losers to Millwall and Aston Villa respectively. In 2006, City again reached the final where they took on Liverpool, but a crushing 3-0 defeat in the first leg made their task all but impossible and despite two goals from Danny Sturridge in the return game, City lost 3-2 on aggregate despite probably being the better side over the two games.

BELOW
Daniel Sturridge celebrates his goal with team-mates during the FA Youth Cup Final, 2006

Zenith Data Systems Cup

A HARK BACK TO SOME TRULY dark days, it's an unfortunate but true fact that the Blues entered some meaningless, awkwardly-named competitions, particularly during the Eighties. While Manchester United competed in prestigious European competition, City attempted to raise much-needed funds by entering cup competitions that were little more than an embarrassment for the City faithful. The Zenith Data was such a competition. In 1990 the Blues played three games in a bid to lift a trophy few were interested in – the sparse crowds were testament to that – beating Middlesbrough 2-1 at Maine Road and

then Sheffield United 2-0 away. Leeds United ended the Blues' interest 2-0 at Elland Road. The following year City went out at the first hurdle in a 3-2 defeat at Sheffield Wednesday, thus ending interest in the doomed competition for good.

The pictures in this book were provided courtesy of

GETTY IMAGES
www.gettyimages.com

PA Photos
www.pa.photos.com

COLORSPORT
www.colorsport.co.uk

Cover concept: Kevin Gardner

Design and artwork by Jane Stephens

Image research by Ellie Charleston

Creative Director: Kevin Gardner

Published by Green Umbrella Publishing

Publishers: Jules Gammond, Vanessa Gardner

Written by David Clayton